# Nationalism
# in Colonial Africa

# Nationalism in Colonial Africa

by
THOMAS HODGKIN

NEW YORK UNIVERSITY PRESS
Washington Square

First published 1956 in Great Britain by Frederick Muller Ltd.
First United States edition 1957

Manufactured in the United States of America

# CONTENTS

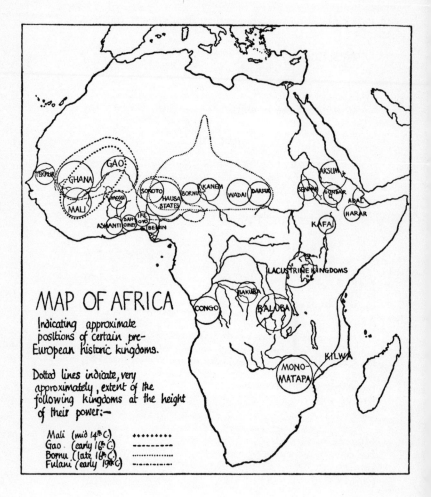

MAP OF AFRICA

Indicating approximate positions of certain pre-European historic kingdoms.

Dotted lines indicate, very approximately, extent of the following kingdoms at the height of their power:—

Mali (mid 14ᵗʰ C.)     ✦✦✦✦✦✦✦✦
Gao (early 16ᵗʰ C.)     ————————
Bornu (late 16ᵗʰ C.)    ················
Fulani (early 19ᵗʰ C.)  —·—·—·—·—

The approximate periods during which the African kingdoms indicated on the accompanying map are believed to have flourished are given below. (Brackets linking the names of two kingdoms indicate an historical connection between them.)

TEKRUR, 10th to 14th centuries.

GHANA (probable capital, Koumbi Saleh), pre-8th to 13th centuries.

MALI, early 13th to late 15th centuries.

GAO (capital of Songhai kingdom), 10th to 13th and 15th to 18th centuries.

MOSSI, 12th to 19th centuries.

ASHANTI (capital, Kumasi), 17th to 19th centuries.

DAHOMEY (capital, Abomey), 17th to 19th centuries.

{ IFE (capital of Yoruba kingdom), pre-13th to 15th centuries.
{ OYO (capital of Yoruba kingdom), 17th to 18th centuries.

BENIN, 15th to 18th centuries.

SOKOTO (capital of Fulani kingdom), late 18th to late 19th centuries.

HAUSA STATES, 12th to late 18th centuries.

{ KANEM, 10th to 14th centuries.
{ BORNU, late 14th to 19th centuries.

WADAI, 15th to 19th centuries.

DARFUR, 15th to 19th centuries.

SENNAR (capital of Fung kingdom), 16th to 19th centuries.

{ AKSUM, 3rd to 8th centuries.
{ GONDAR (capital of Ethiopian kingdom), 17th and 18th centuries.
{ HARAR (Islamic Sultanate), 13th to 19th centuries.

ADAL, 13th to 16th centuries.

KAFA, 14th to 19th centuries.

KILWA, 13th to early 16th centuries.

LACUSTRINE KINGDOMS (Ankole, Ruanda, Urundi, Bunyoro, Buganda, etc.), 15th/16th to 19th centuries.

MONOMATAPA, 15th to 17th centuries.

BALUBA, 17th to 19th centuries.

BAKUBA, 16th to 19th centuries.

CONGO (capital, San Salvador), 15th to 17th centuries.

# ACKNOWLEDGEMENTS

I N writing this book, I have been helped a great deal by a great many people, and especially by these: Professor Asa Briggs of Leeds University; Mr. Kenneth Robinson and Rev. Gervase Mathew of Oxford University; Dr. Kenneth Little, Dr. Michael Banton, and Mr. George Shepperson of Edinburgh University; Dr. Sa'ad-ed-din Fawzi and Saiyid Jamal Mohammad Ahmad of the University College of Khartoum; Mr. Dennis Austin of the University College of the Gold Coast; Mr. George Wigg, M.P.; Mr. David Williams, editor of *West Africa*; Mr. Walter Taplin, former editor of the *Spectator*; Professor Georges Balandier of the University of Paris; Professor Théodore Monod, M. Raymond Mauny, and other members of the staff of the *Institut Français d'Afrique Noire* at Dakar; Professor Gilles Sautter and the *Institut des Études Centrafricaines* at Brazzaville; M. Toussaint and the *Centre d'Étude des Problèmes Sociaux Indigènes* at Elisabethville; Professor Guy Malengreau of the University of Louvain; M. A. Lecointre, editor of *Zaïre*; Dr. James Coleman of the University of California; M. Alioune Diop, editor of *Présence Africaine*; Miss Ruth Schachter; Nana Kobina Nketsia; Mlle. Claude Gérard; Mr. Okoi Arikpo; Mr. Ayo Ogunsheye; Mr. Basil Davidson; Mr. Henry Collins; Mr. F. Le Gros Clarke; Professor Daryll Forde and the library of the International African Institute in London; Miss Audrey James and the library of the Institute of Colonial Studies at Oxford. I have been much helped also by my mother, who typed several chapters and the index; by my sister-in-law, Elisabeth Crowfoot, and my niece, Julian Payne, who drew the maps; and by other members of my extended family. In the case of the map of pre-European Africa, I have drawn on material in Westermann's *Geschichte Afrikas* and in the School of Oriental and African Studies' conference report, *History and Archaeology in Africa*, as well as on the advice of Rev. Gervase Mathew. None of those whom I have mentioned has the least responsibility for what is said here. There are many others not mentioned to whom I am also deeply grateful.

T. L. H.

# INTRODUCTORY

Like other political terms 'the colonial problem' has undergone a change of meaning. In the earlier part of this century writers like J. A. Hobson(1) and Sir Norman Angell(2) were rightly concerned with the competition for colonial possessions as a factor tending to promote, or intensify, conflict between the major European Powers. The practical question which absorbed them was —how to limit, or remove, the rivalries between imperial and would-be imperial Powers, as an evident contributory cause of international wars. The term 'colonial problem' was used also in the period between the two wars in another, secondary sense—the problem of the social ends to be sought, and the administrative methods to be used, by colonial Powers in the territories which they controlled. This, roughly, was the theme of much of the writings of the late Lord Lugard,(3) Lord Hailey,(4) Miss Margery Perham,(5) and others. From this point of departure it was natural to explore such questions as the relative merits of 'indirect' and 'direct' rule, of plantation economies and peasant agriculture; the problems raised by the introduction of European administrative and legal systems, by European commercial penetration and capital investments, by the planting of European settler communities. Chatham House's massive pre-war survey, *The Colonial Problem*, deals with the subject from both these angles—the international and the administrative. But, like most other pre-war studies, it is based on an implicit assumption—that, in some form, European authority over the colonial territories, and particularly colonial Africa, will continue for an indefinite period.

This is an assumption which we are no longer entitled to make. In our generation 'the colonial problem' means, principally, the problem of the relationship between Europe and its outpost communities in Africa, on the one hand, and the indigenous African societies on the other.(6) Put crudely, it means: what adjustments, compromises, surrenders, must the European colonial Powers —and their settlers—make in face of the claims of 'African nationalism'? The explanation of this shift of interest is not hard to find. Reorientations in power relationships mean that the old tensions between 'Have' and 'Have-not' states, and within the circle of 'Haves', though they have not been eliminated, have lost their former urgency. New mechanisms exist for their adjustment. In most of Asia the pre-war European ascendancy has disappeared or is in process of disappearing. Africa remains its last important stronghold. And here the challenge to the old colonial Powers comes less immediately from external influences—the USSR, Asia, the USA—than from within, from the new national movements which post-war Africa has generated. Hence the international aspect of 'the colonial problem' has fallen into the background, and the administrative aspect has lost much of its former interest. For what purpose is served by discussing how you ought to administer territories, if the day after tomorrow you will cease to administer them? It becomes necessary to study African political institutions in precisely the same way as British, French or American institutions are studied—as interesting in themselves, whatever may happen to European power.

The visible signs of these post-war nationalisms are fairly familiar. First, we have become accustomed to a succession of political explosions: in Nigeria and the Gold Coast; in Uganda and Kenya; in the Sudan; in French

West Africa (particularly the Ivory Coast); in the Union of South Africa. Even superficially more tranquil territories—Northern Rhodesia and Nyasaland, the Belgian Congo, French Equatorial Africa and the Cameroons—are admitted by their administrators to be in an eruptive state. Most of the known techniques of seeking political change have been tried out during the past ten years in one region of Africa or another: constitutional agitation; petitions and delegations; appeals to the United Nations; strikes and boycotts; demonstrations and riots; non-co-operation and civil disobedience; terrorism and armed revolt.

Second, during the past few years several new self-governing—if not fully sovereign—States have been brought into being. The Anglo-Egyptian Agreement of February 1953 provided that the Sudan—which has now declared its independence—should draw up its constitution, and decide whether or no it wished any form of constitutional link with Egypt, by the beginning of 1957.(7) Since September 1952 the former Italian colony, Eritrea, has enjoyed the status of an autonomous territory within the federal Ethiopian Empire.(8) The provisions of its 1954 constitution have brought the Gold Coast to the last stage on the road to independence within the Commonwealth.(9) Nigeria—so far at least as its Western and Eastern Regions are concerned—is in an almost comparable position.(10) And 1956 has been noted in the diaries of British West African politicians as the year of decision. In all these States there are now African Prime Ministers presiding over African Cabinets (in Eritrea a 'Chief Executive' presiding over an 'Executive'), responsible to elected African legislatures. Another ex-Italian colony, Somalia, now an Italian Trust Territory, is earmarked for self-government in 1960.(11) The colonial Powers, Britain in particular, have been compelled to modify profoundly the time-schedules for constitutional change on which they were proposing to operate. Constitutions of the early post-war period, like the Burns Constitution in the Gold Coast and the Richards Constitution in Nigeria, which were presented to the public by their designers and salesmen, as up-to-date, durable models, have been quickly sent to the scrap-heap. And, though it has been in certain of the British-controlled territories and the former Italian colonies that the tempo of political change has been most rapid, the shock of these events has unquestionably been felt in French and Belgian Africa.(12)

A third surface expression of the new nationalisms is the interdependence of happenings in the various African territories. Only the Portuguese still seem to keep their colonial peoples relatively insulated. Colonial frontiers no longer act as barriers to the spread of news and ideas. This new sensitivity of Africans in one part of Africa to political developments in another, maybe remote, part was first perhaps evident in 1935–6, at the time of the Italian-Ethiopian War.(13) In these days it is taken for granted that the explanation of a major political event in a given African territory must be sought outside, as well as within, the territory. To take an obvious example: among the links in the causal chain which led to the Buganda crisis of November 1953, and the deposition of Mutesa II, were at least three external facts: revolt and repression in Kenya; the extension of the right to vote to the supposedly 'primitive' Nilotic peoples of the Sudan; and the setting up of the new Rhodesian Federation in response to European settler pressure and in the face of well-organised African opposition. In their different ways these events all tended to promote a hardening of the

Baganda attitude to their own political claims.(14) In a minor key, the modest instalment of constitutional reform introduced by the Belgians in Ruanda-Urundi in 1952, while partly intended to appeal to the United Nations, was also partly a consequence of a gradual political awakening among the Banyarwanda and Barundi, stimulated from Uganda, where tens of thousands of them regularly migrate for work.(15) These influences may operate at long range: the emergence of a self-governing African State in the Gold Coast increases the confidence of Basuto chiefs in the future prospects of Basutoland.

This increased interdependence is partly itself a consequence of vastly improved possibilities of communication. Africans can now speak and listen to one another and to the outside world in a way that has never previously been possible. The development of a nationalist Press, which seeks to stimulate political awareness and activity among the literate and barely literate mass rather than to inform a small élite, has been of special importance. African-controlled journals, like the *West African Pilot* in Nigeria and *Afrique Noire* in French West Africa, have been powerful instruments for the diffusion of the new outlook. Mass-education projects, particularly in British Africa, have widened the circle of the literate.(16) Through broadcasting and films, as well as through newspapers, Africans, even in the remoter small towns and villages, are able to learn about *Apartheid* in the Union of South Africa, Indian independence, the conflicts in Korea and Viet-Nam, the hydrogen bomb. In Nigeria especially there has been a post-war spate of pamphlet literature, comparable with English pamphlet-eering in the 1640s, dealing with every kind of current topic, from polygamy to educational reform. Anti-

colonial ideas imported, partly through returning
students, from a variety of sources—the American gospel
of free enterprise, the Marxist theory of the self-destruc-
tive character of imperialism, the Moslem Brotherhood's
rejection of Western culture, the Gandhist concept of
passive resistance—circulate widely in contemporary
Africa.

Another sign of the times is the appearance of a new
African political leadership which takes itself, and ex-
pects to be taken, seriously.(17) Kwame Nkrumah in the
Gold Coast, Nnamdi Azikiwe and Obafemi Awolowo in
southern Nigeria, Leopold Sédar-Senghor in Senegal,
Félix Houphouet-Boigny in the Ivory Coast, Bartélémy
Boganda in Ubangui-Shari, Isma'il al-Azhari in the
Sudan, are new men, dealers in a new kind of power.
They differ profoundly both from the traditional chiefly
leadership and from the past generation of lawyer-politi-
cians. They combine, perhaps, some of the qualities of
both, in that they enjoy the kind of reverence which the
chief, as the intermediary between God and man, and
symbol of his people's unity and continuity through time,
enjoys in traditional African society; but also the new
kind of authority attaching to those who have mastered
the European's political techniques, and know how to
use them to press African claims. These leaders have the
advantage of being at home in both worlds—the world of
the ancestors, the dance and the market, and the world of
parliamentary debate and the struggle for State power.
Thus they can command popular loyalties and win votes
at elections no less effectively than party leaders in
western Europe. (Jomo Kenyatta, who belongs to the
same category, might be equally successful if he enjoyed
the same degree of liberty.) Judged simply on their political ability, these men do not compare unfavourably with

western European statesmen. A few of them—M. Senghor, for example—are intellectually well above the normal British or French Cabinet Minister standard. It is not unreasonable that they should expect to be treated —as indeed they are beginning to be treated—on terms of equality by the political leaders of Europe, Asia and America.

These profound changes in the post-war political climate of Africa have been noted even by those who like them least. Mrs. Elspeth Huxley, in the preface to the new edition of her life of Lord Delamere, describes them in much the same language as a De Courcy might have used to describe the rise to power of Sir Roger Scratcherd:

"Today's Masai undergraduate at Cambridge might be the son of one of Delamere's aloof and pig-tailed cattle-herds; grandsons of the Kikuyu who bartered with him grain for beads under the watchful eye of an armed *askari* are today's journalists and politicians who claim all Kenya as their own and call for the expulsion of Europeans and full rights of self-government."(18).

While these manifestations of 'African nationalism' are familiar, not much has yet been done by way of explanation and analysis. It is interesting that the only reference to Africa in the 1939 Chatham House Report on *Nationalism* should be concerned with Africa as a recipient of the impact of European nationalism. The embryonic nationalisms which had already begun to develop among certain African peoples are nowhere discussed. Such an omission might have been justified, though doubtfully, in 1939 on the grounds of lack of material. That is not the case today. A considerable amount of interesting material dealing with the history

and institutions of African nationalism now exists—
mainly in the form of specialised studies, scattered about
among a variety of journals, French, American, Belgian,
British, Italian, German, South African. Oddly the
British, who have probably done most among the European nations to stimulate a sense of nationality among
Africans, seem to have written least. The French sources
are perhaps the richest. It is on such material, supple-
mented by a limited amount of personal enquiry, that this
book is based. It does not claim to be more than *proleg-
omena* to a study of African nationalism. My chief concern is to present, in a small compass, the results of other
men's work; to indicate the boundary between what is
known and what is unknown; to suggest connections and
comparisons; and to raise questions which further investi-
gation might help to answer.

Anyone who tries to handle such a theme is bound to
owe a great deal to anthropologists and sociologists, particularly to those among them who have given special attention to the phenomena of social change. But this book
is a study in politics, not in sociology: that is to say, it is
an attempt to describe, and where possible to account for,
the political institutions and ideas of African nationalism, in some relation to their history. The nationalisms
which have developed over the last 150 years—in south-
eastern Europe, in the Arab World, in India and the Far
East—have already been studied from this political standpoint. (19) There seems no reason why a similar method
of treatment should not be usefully applied to the new
nationalisms of Africa. Indeed there is some advantage in
ceasing to regard Africa, as it has sometimes been regarded in the past, as a kind of 'thing-in-itself', the
private preserve of *Africanistes*. This implies an approach which recognises African nationalism, in its many

manifestations, as an historical movement, necessarily and characteristically African, yet revealing definite points of resemblance to the nationalisms that have emerged in other parts of the world. These resemblances seem the more natural if the rise of African nationalism is thought of as the final stage in a chain-reaction, deriving its operative ideas originally from the French Revolution—the doctrine of the Rights of Man interpreted as the Rights of Nations. Thus the revolts of Greeks and Serbs against the Ottoman Empire in the 1820s, and the revolts of West and East Africans against the British and French Empires in the 1950s, belong to the same historical process. But, as M. Alduy has pointed out, it was easier for our ancestors to regard the national movements in the Balkans with 'sympathetic objectivity' than it is for us to show the same attitude to the national movements in contemporary Africa.(20) For the eventual aim of the former was the destruction of the Ottoman Empire; but the eventual aim of the latter is the destruction of our own Western European Empires.

Even in an introductory study of this kind some attention must be paid to the widely different policies pursued by the different European Powers which between them control most of tropical Africa: France, Britain, Belgium and Portugal. For these policies largely determine the framework within which the various African peoples, asserting their new nationalist claims, have to operate. Without at least a brief account of these policies the marked contrasts between the expressions of nationalism in British and French Africa, and in British West and British East Africa, are unintelligible. It is also necessary as a partial explanation of the much less mature, weakly organised nationalisms emerging in Belgian Congo and Ruanda-Urundi; and the apparent non-existence of nationalism in Portuguese Africa. The first part of this book consists, therefore, of a short discussion of the policies of the Powers, with special emphasis, in each case, upon those aspects of policy which are either novel and interesting in themselves, or particularly relevant to an understanding of African political movements and attitudes. The second, and main, part takes the form of an examination of some of the institutions through which African nationalism operates, and of the ideas by which it is influenced. This section is introduced by a sketch of certain features of the 'new towns' of Africa—their physical characteristics, their social life and culture. Just as the Hammonds found it necessary, in order to account for the Chartist movement, to study in detail the state of the towns in the England of the 1840s,(21) so, in order to account for contemporary African nationalism, I believe one must study the new 'proto-industrial' towns—products of the economic revolution which Europe has brought about in Africa. For it is above all in these new urban societies that the characteristic institutions and ideas of African nationalism are born and grow to maturity; and from these centres that they spread to, and influence, 'the bush'. The book concludes with some speculations about the present state and future prospects of African nationalism.

The limitations of such a study are apparent. It is limited by the available material, which is valuable but patchy. It is limited in scope to certain selected aspects of African nationalism. It is limited in time to the post-war situation: the important prehistory and early history of African national movements are referred to only in passing. It is limited geographically to what can broadly be called 'colonial Africa south of the Sahara'. That is to say

Egypt and North Africa, whose main connections are with the Middle East and the Mediterranean, and the Union of South Africa, a sovereign State which 'contains its colonial problem within itself', are regarded as external to colonial Africa.

So far I have attempted no definitions. The terms 'colony' and 'colonial' have been somewhat loosely used: this is difficult to avoid. These words were employed unblushingly in the past by the rulers of 'colonial' States to describe their dependent territories. But since the end of the nineteenth century—originally to avoid international embarrassments and later to escape the criticisms which Lenin and Wilson, Stalin and Roosevelt, launched against the 'colonial system'—there has been a tendency to drop them in polite speech: to regard them rather as the Victorians regarded the word 'trousers'. This changing attitude to language can be correlated with changes in the constitutional relationships between metropolitan and dependent countries. French West and Equatorial Africa are Federations within the complex known as 'Overseas France', a component of the French Republic, *une et indivisible*, itself part of that larger complex, the French Union. Portuguese Africa and, more recently, the Belgian Congo, have become integral parts of the Portuguese and Belgian States. Most of British-controlled Africa consists of Protectorates, not colonies: a difference of status which, as recent events in Uganda, Northern Rhodesia and Nyasaland have shown, still has importance for the more traditionally-minded African nationalists. And if political realities rather than constitutional forms are to be taken into account, the Rhodesian Federation is almost as far on the road to becoming a European-managed 'Dominion' as the Gold Coast and southern Nigeria are to becoming African-managed 'Dominions'.

In addition there are the now sovereign Sudan, and the Trust Territories of Togoland, the Cameroons, Tanganyika, Ruanda-Urundi and Somalia, administered by European Powers on the basis of Trusteeship Agreements with the United Nations. Constitutionally speaking, there are few colonies in contemporary Africa. But though the word 'colony' may lack precise meaning, the word 'colonial' remains useful. I propose to use the latter term—in a morally neutral sense—to refer to a recognised relation of dependence and subordination between an African territory and a non-African Power. (I use this qualification 'recognised', since otherwise Liberia could reasonably be regarded as standing in a colonial relation to the USA.) A 'colonial Power' can then be defined as a state which, through whatever constitutional arrangements, enjoys effective political control over a dependent African territory; a 'colonial people' can be defined as a non-European people, or group of peoples, inhabiting such a territory. ('Effectiveness' is clearly a matter of degree: revolt, as in Kenya, or constitutional change, as in British West Africa, may temporarily limit or finally abolish this control.)

The definition of the term 'African nationalism', which has already occurred fairly frequently, presents greater difficulties. In one sense this book is an attempt at a definition. "Si definitionem requiris, circumspice." But admittedly some preliminary clearing of the ground is necessary.

The Chatham House Report defines 'nationalism' as "a consciousness, on the part of individuals or groups, of membership in a nation, or of a desire to forward the strength, liberty or prosperity of a nation. . . ."(22) In the case of a colonial people particular emphasis tends naturally to be placed on the forwarding of liberty, in the sense of the achievement of self-government. But two questions remain: (1) Which are the African nations? (2) At what stage is it reasonable to describe a movement of colonial protest, or opposition to European authority, as 'nationalist' in respect of its aims and character?

The first question presents fewer puzzles than might appear. It is true, of course, that African 'nationalism' operates, or tries to operate, at a variety of levels: at the level of a particular language-group, or greater tribe— Yoruba, Ewe, Baganda, Banyarwanda, Kikuyu; of a particular colonial territory—Ubangui-Shari, the Gold Coast, Uganda; or Federation—Nigeria; or former colonial territory—Togoland and the Cameroons, of a wider 'trans-territorial' region—*Afrique Noire*, West Africa; and, finally, of 'Pan-Africa'.(23) Effective political organisations have been built up at each of the first three levels, e.g. the Yoruba Action Group, the Gold Coast Convention People's Party and the Pan-French-African *Rassemblement Démocratique Africain*. The last level belongs so far mainly to the world of ideas and projects—those conceived, for example, by Kwame Nkrumah in the Gold Coast and Harry Nkumbulah in Northern Rhodesia— rather than of practical politics. But it is not a peculiarly African phenomenon that, during a period of struggle for independence from foreign rule, the shape of the nations-to-be should remain somewhat cloudy and undefined, or that various competing or coexisting nationalisms, appealing to wider or narrower loyalties, should be thrown up in the process. In the latter half of the nineteenth century and after, Macedonian, Greater Bulgarian and Pan-Slav sentiments and political movements coexisted in south-eastern Europe. During the period of Arab nationalist opposition, first to Turkish and later to British and French rule, one could find layers of Druse, Lebanese,

Greater Syrian and Pan-Arab nationalism, imposed one above the other. Disraeli was aware of this overlapping of nationalisms within the Arab World when, in *Tancred*, he made the Maronite, Francis El Kazin, say:

"If there had been the Syrian nation instead of the Maronite nation, and the Druse nation, and half a dozen other nations besides, instead of being conquered by Egypt in 1832, we should have conquered Egypt ourselves long ago, and have held it for our farm. We have done mighty things truly with our Maronite nation!"

"To hear an El Kazin speak against the Maronite nation," exclaimed Rafael Farah, with a look of horror; "a nation that has two hundred convents."

In contemporary Africa, as in the Balkans and the Middle East at an earlier stage, national movements have their particularist and their universalist aspects. And it would not be surprising if, as in the Balkans and the Middle East, in the short run particularism asserted itself. The loyalties associated with the idea of 'Ghana', *Soudan Français* and *Kamerun*, seem for the moment more powerful than those aroused by the concept of Nigeria, *Afrique Occidentale Française* or a United States of West Africa. There is, moreover, one special difficulty which Africans have to face: little attention was paid, in the original partition of Africa or in its re-partition after the First World War, to effective social groupings; so that peoples who had traditionally enjoyed a certain coherence found themselves divided between the territories of different colonial Powers. The Somalis, divided between British, French and Italian Somaliland, as well as Ethiopia, are a classic example;(24) but the Ewes, distributed over the Gold Coast and British and French Togoland,(25) and the Bacongo, split by the frontiers of

French Moyen-Congo, the Belgian Congo and Portuguese
Angola, (26) are in a comparable situation. In these and
other cases, nationalisms aiming at reuniting peoples
whom European colonisation divided have begun to
assert themselves, making the pattern of African nationalisms more complicated. Particularist tendencies may be
strengthened too by the fact that Africans, unlike Arabs
or South Slavs, lack a common religion and common language, or closely related languages. For the moment the
difficulties in the way of preserving unity in multi-
national, multi-religious Nigeria seem considerable;
while the problems involved in the creation of a wider
union of British, French, Portuguese and Americo-
Liberian West Africans seem of a different order of difficulty. For all that, the late Professor Montagne was wise
to stress the potential attraction of larger African groupings and amalgamations.(27)

The second question is partly a matter of definitions.
My own inclination is to use the term 'nationalist' in a
broad sense, to describe any organisation or group that
explicitly asserts the rights, claims and aspirations of a
given African society (from the level of the language-
group to that of 'Pan-Africa') in opposition to European
authority, whatever its institutional form and objectives.
This is the sense in which the term is normally used in
this book. But there are other possibilities. Mr. Coleman,
to judge from his interesting paper, *Nationalism in
Tropical Africa*, would like to use the word in a much
more restricted sense: to describe only those types of
organisation which are essentially political, not religious,
economic or educational, in character, and which have as
their object the realisation of self-government or independence for a recognisable African nation, or nation-to-
be ('Ghana', Nigeria, *Kamerun*, Uganda). M. Georges

Balandier would seem to incline to the same view when he argues that it is "a kind of misuse of terms" to refer to "any form of organisation, however rudimentary, which escapes from the control of the dominant Powers, any protest against a situation of political inferiority, any movement stimulated by local policies of racial discrimination", as expressions of nationalism.(28)

While, obviously, every terminology has its advantages and disadvantages, to restrict the use of the term in this way seems to me to raise two difficulties. First, it tends to conceal the 'mixed-up' character of African political movements. In a single African territory it is possible to find coexisting a diversity of organisations, of different types, with different objectives, operating at different levels, each in its own way expressing opposition to European control and a demand for new liberties; and to discover a network of relationships between these organisations. For example, in Nigeria during the period of political ferment from 1945 to 1950 there were functioning (among a multitude of other organisations): (1) A typical 'Congress-type' political organisation, claiming independence for the Nigerian 'nation'—the National Council of Nigeria and the Cameroons—some of whose leaders, Dr. Azikiwe included, had at that time Pan-African associations and aspirations. (2) A partially underground, quasi-revolutionary organisation, with certain Messianic features—the Zikist movement. (3) Separatist Churches, such as the National Church of Nigeria and the Cameroons, expressing a greater or less degree of hostility to the European Missions. (4) Tribal associations, such as the Ibo Union, concerned partly with mutual assistance and friendly benefits, partly with modernising and educating the rural areas, and partly with promoting a sense of tribal nationalism. (5) Trade unions, providing a channel not only for pressure for improvements in wages and working conditions, but also for radical criticism of the European-controlled economy, and the palpable differences in living-standards between Africans and Europeans. Most of these various types of organisation possessed links, formal or informal, with one another. Many of them were not concerned, overtly or primarily, with achieving political independence or stimulating a sense of Nigerian nationhood. None the less they were all, in one sense, variations on a single theme; intelligible only in relation to a single historical process, of nationalist awakening, to which they all belonged.

Second, the restricted definition of 'nationalism' seems to imply that nationalism is non-existent in such territories as the Belgian Congo, where no African political organisations aiming at self-government exist, or would be permitted to exist, and where the sense of Congolese nationhood is rudimentary. Yet movements opposing European rule and asserting African rights are at work in the Congo, and have been working for the past generation. The sentiments and beliefs of politically-minded members of the Congolese élite differ very little from those of politically-minded Africans across the frontiers, in Northern Rhodesia or French Equatorial Africa. It would be more accurate therefore to say that the Congo is still in the phase of 'incipient nationalism', as contrasted with the 'mature' or 'developed nationalism' of, say, the Gold Coast: or even that in the Belgian Congo, as in much of French Africa (outside the Trust Territories of French Togoland and the French Cameroons) nationalist aspirations have not yet begun to express themselves in the language of separatism.(29)

# I

## POLICIES OF THE POWERS

THE chief object of this chapter is to consider some of the differences between the African policies of the three major colonial Powers—Britain, France and Belgium—and the different ways in which these policies have affected the growth of African nationalism in the period since the Second World War.(1) But it may be useful to begin by noting certain points of resemblance.

All three Powers have carried a good deal further the process of equipping their territories with the panoply of modern states—*infrastructure* as the French term it: internal and international airlines; road networks; telephone systems; urban electricity schemes; broadcasting services; research institutes, and the like.(2) With this has gone a new emphasis on public investment and economic planning. The French work on the basis of a succession of four-year plans for their overseas territories; the Belgians have a ten-year plan for the Congo and Ruanda-Urundi; and in most British African territories there are ten-year development programmes in operation. Public investment for the period from 1945 to 1952/3 may be estimated as roughly £275 million for French, £160 million for British, and £75 million for Belgian, Africa;(3) and, though many economists would argue this is well below the desirable minimum, it is certainly on a much larger scale than pre-war. New agencies have been set up for pumping loans and grants into colonial territories—the *Fonds d'Investissement pour le Developpement Écono-*

*mique et Sociale des Territoires d'Outre-Mer* (FIDES) in France, Colonial Development and Welfare in Britain; and for spending public funds—the French *Sociétés Mixtes* and the British Colonial Development Corporation. One consequence of economic expansion has been a large increase in the number of European managers and technicians who have been injected into Africa—followed, in French and Belgian Africa, by a crowd of *petits-blancs,* camp followers, who run bars and barbers' shops and beauty parlours in the main centres of population. This swelling of the European communities (with, in some territories, a growth of European-African economic competition) has tended to increase the isolation and self-sufficiency of the European worlds, even in non-settler countries; and thus to intensify antagonism between Europeans and Africans.

One aspect of this growth of public spending has been a quickening in the pace of educational development.(4) This has naturally been most evident in the areas of rapid political change: universal primary education has now been introduced in the Gold Coast, and is projected in western and eastern Nigeria. But elsewhere there are signs of the same general trend. In French West Africa the school population, though still representing only about 10 per cent of the children of school age, has more than doubled since 1946. In the Belgian Congo there are now over a million children, about 50 per cent of the school-age population, attending some kind of school. More important in some ways than the mere fact of expansion has been the tendency to diversification—the development of secondary, technical and adult education of various types, and the effort to make up some of the leeway in girls' education. Especially significant has been the considerable, though uneven, increase in opportunities for university education for students from British and French Africa—about 4,000 of whom are now attending British, French and American universities.(5) At the same time new university institutions have been created in Africa—the University Colleges of the Gold Coast, Nigeria, British East Africa and the Sudan; the projected University College of Rhodesia;(6) the *Institut des Hautes Études* at Dakar; Lovanium, at Kimuenza in the Belgian Congo, affiliated to the Catholic University of Louvain. In varying degrees all three Powers are thus committed to the training of an African governing class.

All three Powers have likewise been compelled to give increasing attention to the problems associated with the transformation of peasants into proletarians and the growth of the new towns: through reforms in labour legislation and the appointment of Labour Officers or *Inspecteurs du Travail*; the improvement of health and hospital services; the first efforts to deal with the enormous problem of urban housing; the provision of at least the rudiments of welfare services—community centres, youth clubs, child welfare clinics, municipal restaurants, an embryonic probation service.(7)

Even in the political field there are certain points of resemblance. Unostentatiously, and without official pronouncements, the three Powers have tended to shift their political support from 'chiefs'—whether traditional rulers or Government nominees—and transfer it to members of the new educated élite. The extent to which this process has occurred varies greatly, of course, from territory to territory, as do the status and influence of those described as chiefs. There are still strongholds of princely power—in northern Nigeria and Ruanda-Urundi, for example. But the decline of the chiefly interest, and the growing prestige of the 'young men', the

Western-educated, the *évolués*, the new middle class, is a common theme of British, French and Belgian literature. This is the class to which the new representative institutions of British and French West Africa and the Sudan (and, to a much more restricted extent, of British East Africa) have presented political opportunities; and which is beginning to express itself through the purely advisory councils of the Belgian Congo.

The changing social and political climate in colonial Africa necessitates a change in administrative attitudes. European administrators (where they still survive)—from Governors-General down to the newest District Officers—have increasingly to be foxes rather than lions. There is less and less room for the administrator who sees his job as being primarily to govern: to preserve law and order, administer impartial justice, increase agricultural production, deal severely with malcontents, agitators and Jacobins, act as a father to his people. The modern administrator has to be a good practical psychologist, with a working knowledge of political theory, from Machiavelli to Lenin; trained in the arts of diplomacy and negotiation; with the adaptability which enables him to turn easily from planning a mass-education campaign to trying to settle a railway strike; who is well aware of his incapacity to control the course of events, and sees it as his main job to grasp the various currents of public opinion, so that, by skilful manœuvring, he may be able during his time to maintain an unstable equilibrium.

There is an obvious explanation of these common characteristics of post-war colonial policies. Certain common influences have been at work: the impact of the Second World War, and the desire of the British, French and Belgian Governments to secure the support of their colonial peoples; the influence of the Left in the Parlia-

ments of the Western democracies in the period immediately following the war; the attitude to the 'colonial
system' of the United Nations—or of the majority of its
member States—which, though frequently deplored by
the colonial Powers, has had the merit of compelling
them to give a public account of their administration;
new pressures and demands arising within colonial
Africa. Indeed, the fact that Portuguese policy appears to
have been so little affected by these new trends is clearly
connected with Portugal's peculiar position, as a state
which did not participate in the war, has not hitherto
been a member of the United Nations, and permits no
open debate or radical criticism in the home country. (8)

The following account of some distinguishing characteristics of French, British and Belgian policies in Africa,
is necessarily brief and selective.

## French Cartesianism

French colonial administrators are in the habit of con-
trasting what they describe as their own 'Cartesian' approach to the problems of African government with the
'Empiricism' of the British. This is one of those neat
generalisations which is only partially true, but has certain practical uses. Of course, the French do not really
begin with a few self-evident axioms about France's relations with French Africa, from which they proceed to
deduce a variety of propositions covering all aspects of
policy and administration. Nor do the British reject all
assumptions and live entirely from hand to mouth. But
the French are certainly more interested in the effort to
make their system coherent and intelligible; and are
more conscious of, and worried about, its actual illogicali-
ties and inconsistencies. And, with their much more centralising habits of thought and methods of government,

they have achieved a measure of uniformity in the pattern of institutions which they have introduced into *Afrique Noire* that is altogether lacking in British Africa. Though even in this there is, inevitably, a gap between theory and practice: political and legal institutions which are formally identical do not in fact work out in the same way in Senegal, with its liberal-socialist tradition, and in Chad, the stronghold of Gaullism.

French pre-war colonial policy can best be understood in terms, not of the conventional text-book distinction between 'Assimilation' and 'Association', but of the contrast between what Mr. Kenneth Robinson has called the policy of Identity and the policy of Paternalism.(9) These two policies bear some relation to the revolutionary-equalitarian and conservative-autocratic phases in French internal history. In French Africa the policy of Identity—"the policy seeking in principle to establish in the colonial country institutions identical with those at home"—can be traced back to the decree of 16 Pluviose, Year II (1792), which proclaimed the abolition of Negro slavery, and declared that "all men, without distinction of colour, domiciled in French colonies, are French citizens, and enjoy all the rights assured by the Constitution."(10) Institutionally, in pre-war Africa, this principle was expressed in the citizen rights—including, after 1848, the right to elect a deputy to the French National Assembly—enjoyed by the African inhabitants of the original *Quatres Communes* of Senegal (St. Louis, Rufisque, Dakar, and—till 1929 when it was absorbed by Dakar—Gorée); in the status of these *Communes de plein exercice*, self-governing municipalities on the French model, with their own elected Mayors and Councils; and, till 1920, in an elected *Conseil Général*, with powers extending over the whole area covered by the *Communes*.

The principle of Identity was also, in part, reflected in the educational system (particularly in French West Africa)—predominantly public, free, secular and conducted in the French language.

With the extension of French power over a vast area of West and Equatorial Africa at the end of the nineteenth century, the policy of Paternalism came to be increasingly adopted and applied; so that the Senegalese *Communes* survived simply as equalitarian islands in an authoritarian sea. Paternalism meant, in effect, a special régime for the mass of Africans who were subjects, not citizens. They were subject to customary law—not the French legal code—administered by the French *Commandant du Cercle* or *Subdivision*; their lives were governed by the system known as the *Indigénat*, which virtually deprived them of the liberties of criticism, association and movement, and gave to the French administrator power to inflict disciplinary penalties, without trial, for a wide range of minor offences; and they were liable to compulsory labour, *travail forcé*, for public, and sometimes private, purposes.(11)

The Brazzaville Conference of February 1944, which set itself to define the post-war basis of relationships between the new France and her overseas territories, was evidently torn between these two principles—Identity and Paternalism—and its final resolutions took, for the most part, the form of a succession of uneasy compromises. (11) But, as it turned out, pressure from the new African parties which emerged after the liberation, and from the metropolitan parties of the Left, was strong enough to push the Fourth Republic much further along the road of Identity than Brazzaville had ever contemplated.

The new dispensation, eventually embodied in the

1947 Constitution, is an interesting example of the elements of consistency and inconsistency in French policy. The pivotal reform was the first *Loi Lamine Gueye* of May 7th, 1946, restated as Article 80 of the Constitution, the 'French Edict of Caracalla', according to which "tous les ressortissants des territoires d'outre-mer ont la qualité de citoyen au même titre que les nationaux français de la metropole ou des territoires d'outre-mer". From this a number of other reforming measures flowed logically enough. If Africans were French citizens, it followed that they could no longer be subject to the special régime of the *Indigénat*; that, though they might remain within the scope of customary law in regard to matters of personal status, in penal cases they must be tried by the French criminal courts; and that they could no longer be liable to compulsory labour. In common with other French citizens they must enjoy the normal rights of meeting and association. As citizens they must be represented in the legislative organs of the Republic, the National Assembly and the Council of the Republic, as well as in the advisory Assembly of the French Union. While the whole conception of the Overseas Territories as integral parts of an indivisible Republic, in which legislation was the exclusive responsibility of the French Parliament, made it impossible to contemplate setting up anything in the nature of local legislative assemblies, the French institution of local government, the *Conseil Général*—already tried out in Senegal—was extended to the whole of French Africa. These *Conseils Généraux*, later renamed *Assemblées Territoriales*, were established in each of the eight Territories of French West Africa, the four Territories of French Equatorial Africa, and the two Trust Territories of Togoland and the Cameroons. At the level of the two

Federations—of West and Equatorial Africa—a new institution, the *Grand Conseil*, was introduced, which, like the *Assemblées Territoriales*, is primarily concerned with economic and financial questions, and has, in principle, control over the annual Budget.(12) Moreover, the concept of equality of citizenship carried with it economic and social implications: Africans would be unable fully to exercise the rights of French citizens if their productivity, standards of living and educational opportunities were vastly inferior to those of Frenchmen. Hence the new insistence on the expansion of public investment, and the invention of FIDES as the instrument for "transforming the overseas territories into modern societies".(13)

It is perhaps an illustration of the Cartesian strain in French policy that this entire programme of logically connected reforms should have been put into operation in one piece, in the years of reconstruction, 1946–7. Since then there have been no changes in fundamentals: only a certain amount of tidying up of the system, usually in response to the pressure of African organisations and politicians, directing their main attack upon particular anomalies in the application of the policy of Identity. Hence the second (1950) *Loi Lamine Gueye*, providing for equality of salaries, terms and conditions for African and European civil servants; the *Code du Travail*, of December 15th, 1952, whose object was to bring the labour legislation of the Overseas Territories as closely as possible into line with that of metropolitan France;(14) and the new legislation whereby it is proposed to extend to the larger French African towns the status of *Commune de plein exercice*, hitherto enjoyed only by the Senegalese Communes.(15)

Some of the implications of post-war French policy for African nationalism are immediately obvious. On the one hand a sufficient degree of civil and political liberty now exists for African political parties and trade unions to function, African newspapers to be published; within limits, opposition and criticism are tolerated. On the other hand, the pull of the metropolitan axis is so strong that African political parties tend, in one way or another, to become linked with metropolitan parties; African leaders, once they become deputies or senators, are involved in the play of metropolitan politics; African trade unions are for the most part organised within the framework of the French trade union movement, and reproduce the divisions between CGT, CFTC and Force Ouvrière. The ideas of nationalism compete with, or are modified by, the theories which France exports—Communism and Gaullism, Existentialism and Neo-Thomism.

Less obvious is the fact that French policy, while appearing coherent and systematic, contains within itself a number of contradictions. Nationalism in post-war French Africa has developed to a large extent around the effort to resolve these contradictions. They might be summarised somewhat as follows:

| | |
|---|---|
| 1. The conception of the universality of French civilisation—an open society, in which no attention is paid to race or nationality, and men are valued simply in relation to merit and intelligence. | 1. The fact that the French who reside in French Africa, official and unofficial (and particularly the *petits-blancs*) are as liable as any other Europeans to develop the typical European stereotypes ('Africans are children', etc.), and to exhibit symptoms of racial arrogance. |

2. The principle, embodied in the Constitution of the Fourth Republic, that French Africans, as citizens, enjoy equal political rights with metropolitan Frenchmen.

2. The system of the 'Dual College'—operative throughout French Africa, except for Senegal, Mauretania and Togoland—the effect of which is to give a much heavier weight to the votes of metropolitan Frenchmen than to the votes of Africans.(9)

The wholly inadequate representation of French Africa in the French Parliament—having regard simply to its population as compared with that of France. The logic of equality should imply 390 African deputies in the National Assembly, instead of the present 29.(16)

3. The principle of popular participation in the processes of government, expressed in a three-tiered system of representative institutions (at the level of Territory, Federation and Republic), with near-universal suffrage.

3. The fact that none of these institutions is such as to give Africans effective control of, or a substantial share in, *executive* power in French Africa. The system provides for representative, but not responsible, government. Hence the Administration appears as a quasi-independent power, much influenced still by the principle of Paternalism.(17)

4. The idea of expanding opportunities for higher education, with a view to building up a growing African élite, capable of carrying out administrative and specialist functions, on equal terms with Frenchmen.

4. The fact that the administrative hierarchy remains dominated by Frenchmen; that little progress has in fact been made with 'Africanisation', either in Government or business; and that career prospects for the University-educated African élite are restricted.

5. The recognition that equality of political rights has limited value, unless accompanied by an effort to abolish gross inequalities of economic standards and opportunities; with the implication that France must spend heavily on the development of African economies.

5. The fact of the extreme continuing inequality of African and European living-standards—"the average income of a French peasant is Fr. 219,000 per annum, and of a French West African peasant Fr. 18,000".(17)

## British Empiricism

On what grounds is British colonial policy consistently referred to as 'empirical'? It would be difficult to maintain that the mind of the British Colonial Office is a *tabula rasa*, capable only of receiving and recording impressions. There is an *a priori* element in British thinking about colonial questions as well as in French, though probably it is less explicit. "British practice doubtless pivots on precedent rather than on principle. . . . But both precedents and principles lead their addicts to much the same destination in the long run; and, as often as not, in the short run. Precedents end in systems. They are only principles in reverse."(18) What is partly meant by describing British policy as 'empirical' is that it is normally developed piecemeal, in relation to specific situations, or as a means of solving specific problems. For example, the policy of rapidly transferring political power in West Africa to independent or autonomous African Governments was certainly not contemplated by the Labour Party when it took office in 1945. Yet it is this aspect of post-war British policy that is regarded by most foreign commentators as having the most far-reaching implications for colonial Africa. In practice the turning-point seems to have occurred in 1948, after the February disturbances in the Gold Coast, and the acceptance by the British Government of the Watson Commission's Report, with its radical criticisms of the Gold Coast 1946 Constitution, and its no less radical conclusion:

"The Constitution and Government of the country must be so reshaped as to give every African of ability an opportunity to help to govern the country, so as not only to gain political experience but also to experience political power. We are firmly of opinion that anything less than this will only stimulate national unrest."(19)

This statement contains the germ of the 'new model' colonial policy which Britain has been applying, with variations and differences in tempo, in Nigeria and Sierra Leone as well as in the Gold Coast since 1948-9. Its essential characteristics are—the transformation of the traditional forms of colonial Legislative Council into democratically elected Parliaments (in some cases with an Upper House to provide an outlet for chiefs); universal or manhood suffrage; the introduction of a Ministerial system; an effort to speed up the process of 'Africanising' the Administration, with the rapid expansion of education—particularly higher education—which this involves; the requirement that British officials shall regard themselves as servants of African Ministers, not as members of a Ruling Institution—with the eventual implication that control of the Public Service is transferred from the Colonial Office to the new national Governments; the progressive abandonment of the concept of the 'Native Authority' as the basis of local government, and the substitution of the concept of the—predominantly elected —Local Authority;(20) the acceptance of the principle that these constitutional reforms are preliminaries to the granting of full independence within the Commonwealth at an early, if undefined, date.

Since spectators often see more of the game than the players, it is worth considering how this 'new model' British policy looks to French observers. M. J.-L. Simonet, writing in *Politique Etrangère*, makes the following interesting points.(21) First, British policy in West Africa has in fact been running closely parallel to French—in that the operative pre-war principle of Paternalism (in its classic British form of 'Indirect Rule') has been replaced by the principle of Identity (in the form of the export of British parliamentary, Cabinet and Local Government institutions.) Second, regarded from the standpoint of *Realpolitik*, what this policy amounts to is a realistic decision to withdraw British support from the declining chiefly interest, and transfer it to the rising African middle class and the new educated élite. Third, it is evident that 'self-government within the Commonwealth' is far from involving any total surrender of British power in West Africa. Britain's—relative—commercial and military ascendancy, and her long imperial experience, are sufficient to ensure, for the present at any rate, that the emerging West African 'Dominions' remain well within the British orbit. Fourth, British policy is able to show this degree of flexibility, and make large political concessions to the nationalist-minded African middle class, in West Africa, because of the absence of *colons*. In East and Central Africa, where there are well-organised, clamant settler minorities, British policy is exposed to the same embarrassments, and involved in the same duplicities, as French policy in *colon*-ridden North Africa.

This last point suggests a second sense in which British colonial policy might be described as 'empirical'. A less polite word would be 'opportunistic'. Partly, of course, because of the geographical spread-outness of British Africa, and the diversity of the political situations within the various territories—and partly because the position of a British Secretary of State for the Colonies in relation to his Colonial Governors resembles that of a mediaeval king in relation to his great feudatories—British post-war policy often appears, both to Europeans and Africans, as lacking any kind of internal consistency. It seems to be little more than a succession of unco-ordinated responses to different types of stimulus. In West Africa well-organised nationalist pressure, and absence of settlers, give rise to a policy of 'self-government within the Commonwealth'. In the Sudan the same kind of internal political situation, with the added factor of Egyptian external pressure, lead to an acceptance of the idea of a less gradual transfer of power and total independence. In Uganda, where the national movement is at an earlier stage of development, and East African settler interests are a background factor to be reckoned with, tentative, hesitant steps towards a 'West African' policy begin to be taken. In Kenya, and in the Central African Federation, where the settler interest is sufficiently powerful to insist on the recognition of its claim to maintain European 'leadership' (and African nationalism is still relatively immature), some variant of the policy of Paternalism is still applied—either directly by a colonial Government, or by a semi-independent European Government.

The conflict between the principles implicit in Britain's 'West African' and 'East and Central African' policies might be stated in another way. The theory by which the policies known as 'Partnership', the creation of a 'multi-racial State', and the like, are commonly justified is essentially Burkian: that in a representative assembly what should be represented is not individuals, but interests—the great Estates of the Realm; ability must be well represented, and property, particularly, landed property, and property "in great masses of accumulation", which "form a natural rampart about the lesser properties in all their gradations". Whereas:

"The occupation of a hairdresser, or of a working tallow-chandler, cannot be a matter of honour to any person—to say nothing of a number of other more servile employments. Such descriptions of men ought not to suffer oppression from the state; but the state suffers oppression, if such as they either individually or collectively, are permitted to rule."(22)

Translated into African terms, this means that the basis of representation must be *communal*. The European community (in other words, the landed interest, the commercial interest and the mining interest); the Asian community, where it exists (which is another section of the commercial interest); and the African community (which is predominantly a peasant and labouring interest)— these must be separately represented in the Legislature (and, where non-European participation is permitted, in the Executive). Because ability and property are distributed in inverse proportion to numbers, there must be a heavy weighting of European, and to a less degree Asian, representation. Otherwise ability and property would be swamped by numbers; and the State would 'suffer oppression' because it would be ruled by 'working tallow-chandlers'. Carried a stage farther, this communal theory of the State can also be used to justify the organisation of public and social services—schools, hospitals and the like—on a communal basis.

Britain's 'West African', and more particularly its 'Gold Coast', policy on the other hand is based on traditional liberal-democratic theory—the Benthamite conception that, though men do indeed differ in respect, not only of ability and property, but also of moral worth, these differences should be regarded as politically irrelevant; since there is no known method of trying to ensure that public policy expresses the general interest otherwise than by granting to each individual as nearly as possible equal rights to take part in the processes of election and government.

The antinomies underlying British policy in Africa, which have tended to stimulate the growth of nationalism, can perhaps be summarised as follows:(23)

1. The liberal conception of the devolution of power from Westminster and Whitehall to the local inhabitants of a dependent territory—the 'Durham formula': implying, in West Africa, the Sudan, and possibly Uganda, the concession of self-government to nascent African nations.

1. The same formal process of devolution of power in Kenya and the Central African Federation, involving in practice a directly contrary policy—the concession to immigrant (and primarily European) minorities of increasing political authority over the nascent African nations; whose leaders naturally appeal to West African experience to support their political claims.

2. The institution of the Legislative Council, which has been developed in all major African territories, and appears to contain the germ of a national parliament.

2. The fact that, in East and Central Africa (and, till recently, in West Africa), the Legislative Council has represented interests, or Estates, rather than persons; and has failed to provide Africans with—(a) representation commensurate with their numbers in the community; (b) an electoral system through which they could enjoy the experience of choosing their own rulers; (c) an effective measure of executive and administrative power. Hence the tendency of African nationalists to seek to transform the Legislative Council from an Estates-General into a popularly elected National Assembly.

3. The conception of 'Indirect Rule', i.e. of local government as resting in the hands of traditional rulers— Native Authorities—operating within the framework of a British-controlled administration: the system depending for its success upon relations of sympathy and mutual respect between British administrator and African chief.(24)

3. The progressive weakening of the influence of traditional rulers, with the rise of an African middle class, whose status depends on wealth and education, not on lineage; who tend to reject traditional authority as unenlightened, incompetent and British-inspired; and who, as a politically conscious, pushing bourgeoisie, tend to be regarded with less sympathy and respect by the administrator than the 'non-political' gentlemanly chief.

4. The relative freedom enjoyed by the Missions in the field of education; and the creation, both by the Missions and by colonial Governments, of a few great grammar schools; in which the institutions of British public schools—houses, fagging, the prefectorial system, out-of-school societies, Greek plays—have been largely reproduced, and the notion of 'education for leadership' has been operative.(25)

4. The fact that this African élite, though educated for leadership, has—except where the principle of African self-government has been conceded—been largely excluded from the exercise of genuine leadership. Hence the present generation of nationalist leaders in British Africa is mainly drawn from those who have learned in their schools the value of national tradition, the need for collective action, the virtue of resistance to authority; and have applied these lessons to their own situation.

5. The principle that British Africans can expect to enjoy certain basic liberties: to organise for political and industrial purposes; to make speeches and write articles; to move freely within their own countries and travel abroad; and, generally, that nationalist activities are tolerated (in a sense in which they are not in Belgian, Portuguese, or even French, Africa—contrast the attitudes to nationalists in British and French Togoland and the Cameroons).

5. The actual legal and administrative restrictions (varying according to territory and circumstances) imposed by colonial Governments upon nationalist leaders and organisations—through sedition laws, states of emergency, control over migration, police surveillance, etc. (Nationalists, however, realise that, in the British tradition, imprisonment may often be a necessary stage on the road to political power; it was, after all, neither Kwame Nkrumah, nor Jawarhalal Nehru, but John Hampden, who invented the notion of 'Prison Graduate'.)

## Belgian Platonism

Belgians also sometimes claim that their colonial policy is 'empirical'. It has none the less in the past been based upon reasonably definite principles, though these are now being subjected to a process of examination and doubt.(26)

Belgians, as they themselves are apt to point out, are essentially a nation of townspeople—a 'bourgeois' nation —in whose history the self-governing commune has played an important part; whose paintings reflect the esteem in which the prosperous burgher, the civic dignitary, the comfortable middle-class family circle, have traditionally been held. Internal differences and disagreements—between *Flamands* and *Wallons*, between Catholics and Anti-clericals—are real enough, and these are exported to the Congo. But they are normally overlaid by a common belief in what are sometimes regarded as Protestant values—material success, thrift, self-help, domestic decency and comfort, respectability; in the Calvinist gospel of work; and in the small monogamous property-owning family as the pivot of society. To be 'civilised' means to accept, and act upon, these moral beliefs. Thus one idea which, in spite of deviations, has profoundly influenced—and continues to influence—Belgian policy is the idea of 'civilising' the Congolese, in the sense of training them to be good burghers, organising their lives and behaviour on the basis of Belgian middle-class values.

Belgian policy has, however, been pulled in a somewhat different direction by another historic fact. The Congo Free State was created in 1885, largely by the efforts of Leopold II and Henry Morton Stanley. It was not until 1908 that it was transformed into a Belgian colony. Hence it was never, like Senegal or the Gold Coast, exposed to the liberal currents of early nineteenth-century colonial theory. When the Congo was born the prevailing ideas were those of late nineteenth-century imperialism, summarised in the title of M. Pierre Ryckmans' classic—*Dominer pour Servir*. The principles of European authority and African subordination, and of the absolute division between the European and African worlds, were taken for granted. "Except for certain fundamental liberties, borrowed from the Belgian Constitution, . . . natives and non-natives are under juridical régimes completely distinct from each other; they are not under the same civil or penal laws, the same social and economic laws, or the same administrative regulations."(27) This legal division between Europeans and Africans was reflected—in the Congo as in other African territories where the same beliefs were operative—in an entirely separate organisation of education and the social services; in the separation between European and African towns; and in a variety of barriers, both legal and customary, in the way of social intercourse. True, by a legal provision dating back to 1895, it was theoretically possible for 'civilised' Africans to become *immatriculés*, and thus enjoy the same civil rights as Europeans. But this was of little practical consequence. In practice the only method by which an African could escape from his socially subordinate status, and achieve a measure of equality with Europeans, was through the priesthood.

A third formative influence upon Belgian policy has been the Missions—above all the Catholic Missions. According to the Government's admirable statistics, in 1954, out of a total Congo population of a little over twelve million, 3,455,084 were Catholics and 704,254 were Protestants. There were in that year over a quarter of a million Catholic, and about 50,000 Protestant, baptisms. There were 4,978 European Catholic, and 1,357 Protestant, missionaries—in all about 7 per cent of the total European population (including children). Until very recently African education has been a monopoly of the Missions. In 1954 there were 743,841 children in grant-aided, and 292,926 children in non-grant-aided Mission schools.(28) But it is not only when measured in these spectacular, but possibly inflated, quantitative terms that the Missions represent a powerful force. Through their teaching and preaching, their rituals and ceremonial, their pastoral and social work, their network of satellite associations, their range of vernacular periodicals and journals, they exercise, or seek to exercise, a large measure of control over African minds. Again, this is particularly true of the Catholic Missions, which have since 1906, and even earlier, enjoyed a special relationship with the State; and till 1946 were alone entitled to receive Government grants. Traditionally this policy, of using the Missions as the chosen instruments of African education, has been justified, partly on the ground of cheapness; but primarily because, it is argued, only in this way can education be given a positive moral purpose.(29)

It is a commonplace that, if spiritual power in the Congo rests with the Missions, temporal—or at the least economic—power rests with the great concessionary companies—*Union Minière du Haut-Katanga, Forminière, Huileries du Congo Belge,* and the like. Admittedly, it is something of an historical accident that Belgium should have found itself obliged to take over a system whose main framework was constructed by Leopold II, at a time when he ruled the Congo as a personal autocrat, largely as a device for making his colony pay—as well as ensuring that it paid him. However, the concessionary system has now become an integral part of the régime. Its influence has been profound. It accounts, partly, for the existence of a much larger proletariat in the Congo than in most of colonial Africa. "In 1953 about 25 per cent of the population was to be found outside the native areas and in the 'extra-customary' centres of population. This figure represents roughly 37 per cent of the taxpayers. . . ."(27) It explains also the large part which the companies, thanks to their substantial contribution to the national revenue, play in the shaping of general policy. And it accounts for the development of the policy of paternalism, whereby "the workers obtain from the companies lodging, food, clothing, education, medical care, even amusements. Nothing is left to their own initiative, and they suffer from this benevolent guardianship, which takes from them the very feeling of liberty itself."(27)

Thus Paternalism, the officially recognised principle on which Belgium's traditional policy has been based, has a threefold origin: the Catholic conception of society as a hierarchy, in which the ruling element is responsible for providing the conditions for a 'good life' for the ruled; the large corporation's idea of workers' welfare as a means to good industrial relations and maximum output; and the colonial Government's view—that it is desirable and politic to concentrate upon the effort to increase the material prosperity of the mass, and to equip them, through education, to play a useful, if subordinate, part, in a modern society, before any moves are made to train an African élite or grant political rights. Hitherto Paternalism has acted as a unifying principle, in relation to which State, Church and Business have been able to harmonise their—sometimes divergent—interests. One practical consequence has been that Congolese have on the whole been able to enjoy a higher standard of social services—through an efficiently organised network of hospitals and clinics, *foyers*, community centres, housing agencies, labour inspectorate, etc.—than exists elsewhere in colonial Africa. At the same time their lives have probably been subjected to more thorough-going regulation and supervision by Europeans—whether as administrative officers, employers and managers, or missionaries—than any other people in colonial Africa.

I have described the theory on which Belgian colonial policy is based as 'Platonism' because of its resemblance to the argument of the *Republic*. ('Paternalism', clearly, is a word of wider application.) Platonism is implicit in the sharp distinction, social and legal, between Belgian philosopher-kings and the mass of African producers; in the conception of education as primarily concerned with the transmission of certain unquestioned and unquestionable moral values, and intimately related to status and function; in the belief that the thought and behaviour of the mass is plastic, and can be refashioned by a benevolent, wise and highly trained élite; that the prime interest of the mass is in welfare and consumer goods—football and bicycles—not liberty; and in the conviction that it is possible, by expert administration, to arrest social and political change.

None the less, change has occurred. Below I have tried to indicate schematically some of the dilemmas with which Belgian policy has been faced in the post-war climate of the Congo and Ruanda-Urundi.

1. Belgian emphasis upon economic expansion, involving not only mining and cash-crops but also secondary industries; with its social consequences—the growth of a prosperous Congolese middle class, a class of skilled workers, and a swollen unskilled proletariat; the encouragement given to Congolese, above all in Leopoldville and the great towns, to think and act as Economic Men.

1. The lack of political outlets for these new classes: no political parties; no independent African trade Unions; no unsupervised African Press—(*La Voix du Congolais*, M. Bolamba's lively monthly, is edited from a Government office): instead, the effort to provide a variety of shock-absorbers—*conseils d'enterprise*, welfare schemes, Mission-sponsored clubs, etc.—inadequate substitutes for civil liberty.(30)

2. The concept of a *Communauté Belgo-Congolaise*, within which *racisme* is outlawed, and Europeans and *Indigènes* work harmoniously together for the ends of of maximum production, higher living-standards, and the good life.

2. The continuance of racial differentiation between Europeans and *Indigènes* in a variety of fields—civil rights, education, medical services, town-planning, etc.—justified on the ground of cultural differences, but increasingly resented by Congolese *évolués*.*

* The Belgian authorities, it should be said, are well aware of the anomalies of the present situation. The 1947 Sohier Committee recommended that 'Europeanised' Africans should enjoy in every respect the same status as Europeans. But the Congo Administration was unwilling to commit itself to so radical a policy, and decided, in 1952, merely to extend the provisions of the Civil Code to 'civilised' Africans. Holders of the *Carte de Merite Civique* also enjoy certain minor privileges; and there has, since 1952, been some administrative loosening up, in such matters as railway travel, social intercourse between European and African towns, etc.(31)

3. The maintenance of a firm alliance between State and Church, and the enjoyment by the Missions of quasi-monopolistic control of African education, designed in the main to fit the Congolese for practical and subordinate functions.

3. Among the mass of Congolese the survival of old, and the development of new, forms of heresy—Kimbanguism, *Kitawala*, etc.—as protests against the authority of the Establishment. Among the Congolese élite the growth of a demand for secular and higher education, only partially met by—(a) the admission of a few 'civilised' African children to European *Athénées* (*Lycées*); (b) the creation of the first *écoles laïques;* (c) the founding of the Catholic University College of Lovanium, and the State College of Elisabethville.

4. The principle of extreme centralisation: the Provinces are governed from Leopoldville; Leopoldville is governed from Brussels— in effect by the *Ministère des Colonies,* advised by the *Conseil Colonial,* a body of elder statesmen; while the inhabitants of the Congo— European as well as African —take no effective part in the governing process.

4. The growth of centrifugal forces within the Congo — a consequence partly of its wartime dissociation from Belgium; partly of the rapid post-war growth of its European population (90,000 in 1954, 0·7 per cent of the total, as in Kenya), and particularly of its European *colons* (about 7,000), whose associations and leaders are autonomist in outlook, and press for internal self-government on the Rhodesian model; partly, too, a consequence of increasing political awareness, and demands for representation, among the Congolese *évolués.*

(So far the Belgian response to these pressures has been to retain executive power firmly in the hands of the Administration, while permitting the use of the advisory *Conseil du Gouvernement* and *Conseils de Province* as outlets for *colon* and Congolese opinion.)

5. The belief that the Congo (like Plato's Republic) can avoid corruption and revolution if it is insulated from the outside world.

5. The fact that the Congo, lying in the centre of Africa, and a focus of trans-African communications, is necessarily exposed to the impact of new ideas from various quarters: from French Africa (via Leopoldville, in particular); from Rhodesia (through the Katanga); from Uganda (via Ruanda-Urundi); from the Sudan and the Moslem world; as well as from Europe and America; while Ruanda-Urundi, as a Trust Territory, receives periodic shocks from the United Nations.(32)

*Variables*

It is worth trying to indicate some of the main aspects of the colonial situation and colonial policy which affect the development of nationalism in Africa—the variables with which variations in the stage which nationalism has reached, and the forms through which it is expressed, can to some extent be correlated. For example:

1. The scale, tempo and direction of economic development, with its social consequences—urbanisation, and the growth of new classes (commercial, professional, wage and salary earning, etc.), conscious of new needs and asserting new claims. (It is not only the question *how much* economic development, but also *what kind* of development, that is important: e.g. a prosperous independent Ashanti cocoa-farmer is more likely to be conscious of 'rights', and in a position to assert them, than a worker on the plantations of *Huileries du Congo Belge*.)

2. Communications: the level of development of railways, roads, internal air services, posts and telecommunications, and their availability for use by Africans; the territory's relationship to the main trans-African and international routes. (The spread of nationalist ideas along the main railway lines is a common phenomenon, e.g. in the French Cameroons, the Belgian Congo, Kenya; and great international airports—Dakar, Kano, Leopoldville, Khartoum—seem especially sensitive to external political influences.)

3. Western education—its spread, organisation and character: in particular, such aspects as the possibility of access to higher education (including access to European and American universities); the relative emphasis upon 'academic' and 'vocational' studies; the nature of Government-Mission relationships, and the attitude of Missions to their work.

4. The policy of the colonial Government in regard to such questions as:

(*a*) European (and Asian) immigration and settlement: the extent to which non-African minorities are permitted to acquire land and carry on business activities; to introduce industrial or social colour-bars; to influence or control legislation and policy-making.

(*b*) Traditional Authorities: whether these have been preserved with the minimum of modification (as in Buganda, or the Fulani Amirates of northern Nigeria); preserved, but with substantially reduced powers (as in the Gold Coast); or effectively eliminated (as in most of French West Africa).

(*c*) Representative institutions—central and local: their scope and powers (whether legislative, as in British territories; financial, as in French; or merely advisory, as in Belgian); the extent of African participation in these bodies, and whether through nomination or election; where electoral systems exist, the basis of the franchise and methods of election.

(*d*) Civil liberties: the degree to which Africans enjoy generally recognised democratic rights—of meeting, association, publication, movement: in particular, the degree of toleration shown by the colonial Government to independent African political organisations and an independent Press.

(*e*) Administration: the extent to which posts carrying authority in the public service (as well as in the private sector—Missions, commerce, industry) are monopolised by Europeans; or, alternatively, a policy of partial or total 'Africanisation' is pursued. (In Africa, as in other colonial territories in the past, the demand for access to senior administrative posts is one of the first to be raised by the nationalist élite.)

5. The influence of the United Nations, both upon colonial policy and upon African attitudes and demands.(33) (In the Trust Territories the fact that eventual self-government or independence is the acknowledged aim of the system, the impact of United Nations Visiting Missions, and the right of petition, tend—in varying degrees—both to liberalise the behaviour of the administering

Power and to stimulate African political movements.)

An estimate of the values to be given to such variables can make the development, or lack of development, and characteristic forms, of nationalism in a given territory more intelligible. For example, in the Gold Coast and southern Nigeria, the presence of such factors as a sizeable, relatively prosperous, middle class, reasonably easy access to higher education for a small élite, the absence of important non-African minorities (with the possible exception of Lebanese), a substantial measure of freedom of speech and association, a long-established African Press, and a tradition of African participation in the Legislature, one might expect to find African nationalist activities mainly directed towards the creation of 'modern' organisations—political parties, trade unions, and the like. In Kenya, on the other hand, or in the Belgian Congo, where European *latifundia* have transformed free peasants into agricultural labourers, European and Asian commercial activities have checked the development of an African middle class, opportunities for higher education have been much more restricted, civil liberties circumscribed or non-existent, no effective African Press has established itself, and such legislative or advisory bodies as exist have been dominated by non-Africans—nascent African nationalism might be expected to express itself rather through tribal organisations, reasserting traditional claims and values, apocalyptic religious movements, or underground resistance and revolt.

Two points, however, need to be emphasised. First, none of these factors acts in a simple or uniform way. The preservation of traditional authorities may in one context—northern Nigeria, for example—provide restraints upon the growth of nationalist sentiments and organisaions; in another context—Buganda—a traditional ruler may serve for a time as a nationalist rallying-point. A European settler minority may, as in Kenya, seem to block the realisation of even moderate nationalist aims; at the same time it may, unwittingly, teach African nationalists a good deal about political organisation and techniques. Second, colonial policies and systems are only part—though an important part—of the environment within which nationalist movements occur, develop and operate. Other external influences, largely outside the control of the colonial Power—Islam, for example—also affect the situation. So do the pre-European history, and its traces in contemporary culture of the various African peoples.

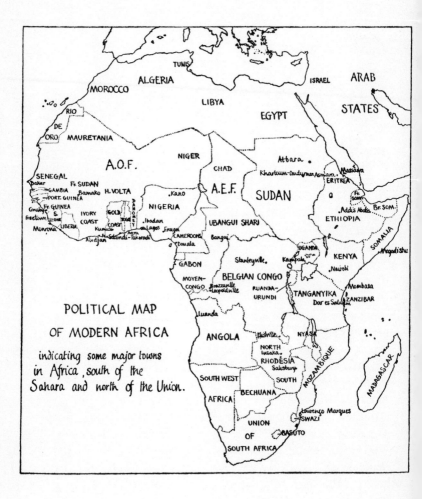

POLITICAL MAP
OF MODERN AFRICA

indicating some major towns
in Africa, south of the
Sahara and north of the Union.

# I

## THE NEW TOWNS

"Qui n'a pas été à Kumassi n'ira pas au Paradis."

THE point is often made that the new towns of Africa act as solvents, weakening traditional social ties and loosening the hold of traditional beliefs and values. This is partly true: but the positive function of towns is no less important. By providing opportunities for a greater degree of specialisation, towns enable men (and women) to acquire new skills and powers. By mixing men from a variety of social backgrounds they make possible the discovery of new points of contact and interest. Around these interests there develops a network of new associations, through which for the first time men come to think of their problems as social rather than personal; as capable of solution by human action rather than part of the natural order. Thus African towns have this two-fold aspect: seen from one standpoint, they lead to a degradation of African civilisation and ethic; seen from another, they contain the germs of a new, more interest-ing and diversified, civilisation, with possibilities of greater liberty. Europeans, and Africans who think like Europeans, tend to be preoccupied with the former aspect; the mass of Africans with the latter. In this and the following chapter an effort will be made to do justice to both.

The town is not a new phenomenon in tropical Africa.

In parts of pre-European Africa (in the western Sudan in particular) urban communities existed. Jenne, Walata, Timbuktu, Gao, Kano, had many centuries of continuous history before the period of European colonisation.(1) They were towns in the normal sense of the term: "coherent, autonomous societies, centres of commerce, government and intellectual activity; inhabited by a population detached from the land—burghers, not peasants".(2) What is new—a product essentially of the colonial epoch—is the great amorphous squalid *agglomération urbaine*: Dakar, Abidjan, Sekondi-Takoradi, Accra, Lagos, Douala, Brazzaville, Leopold-ville, Kampala, Nairobi. These new African towns are as unlike Timbuktu as Stoke-on-Trent is unlike Chichester.

The comparison of these towns with the new industrial towns of northern England in the 1840s is one that immediately suggests itself—as regards not only their physical appearance and social conditions, but also the ideas which underlie their disorder. "The dissolution of mankind into monads, of which each one has a separate principle, the world of atoms, is here carried to its utmost extreme."(3) But in one essential respect at least mid-twentieth-century Dakar and Lagos differ from mid-nineteenth-century Leeds and Manchester: the cause of their existence, the basis of their economic life, is not factory industry but commerce. They have been brought into being to meet the needs of European trade. Their main function is to drain out of Africa its ground-nuts, palm-products, coffee, cocoa, cotton, minerals; and to pump into Africa European consumer goods—cloth, kerosene, bicycles, sewing-machines. Their focal points—substitutes for the cathedrals and guildhalls of mediaeval

Europe, the mosques and bazaars of the Arab world—are the warehouses of the great European commercial houses —UAC and UTC, SCOA and FAO. Hence the fact that so many of the new towns—the first six in my random list —are also seaports. Of the others, Brazzaville and Leopoldville are twin Congo ports, transferring their river traffic to the twin railways which link them with their respective seaports—Pointe-Noire and Matadi. Kampala is primarily a great cotton market—just as Kumasi is a cocoa market; Kano a ground-nut market; and Elisabethville a copper market. Often the new towns were entirely European inventions—Abidjan, Leopoldville, Nairobi, for example: sometimes—like Lagos, Douala and Kampala—they were set alongside of, and eventually swallowed, the capital and trading-centre of a traditional African kingdom. Kano is something of a special case: an ancient walled Hausa city, whose pre-European prosperity was based upon the trans-Saharan trade, now transformed and inflated into a new town (within which the old survives)—with its main orientation reversed, so that it now looks south, down the railway to Lagos—a nerve-centre of the new system of air communications across Africa.

M. Richard-Molard brings out clearly the fundamentally commercial outlook of most African towns. Of Kaolack, a secondary port of Senegal, he says: "It is to ground-nuts that the town owes its whole existence; its entire cosmopolitan population—of middlemen and brokers, dealers in cloth, lorry-drivers, garage proprietors, hotel-keepers, *marabouts*, jobbers of all descriptions, officials, bank clerks, domestic servants, labourers and dockers: a town so concentrated upon ground-nuts that it forgets to think about itself, or even for the present to become a real town at all."(2)

The spectacular growth of the new towns during the post-war period is connected with another fact: that the great commercial centre is also an administrative centre. Either—like Abidjan, Kumasi or Elisabethville—a regional capital; or—like Dakar, Lagos, Leopoldville—the capital of a colonial State. With the increasing complexity and expanding field of operations of the administrative machine, and the increase in Government spending, there has gone—particularly during the immediate post-war years—a building boom: a drive to erect new Government offices, schools, hospitals, post offices, telephone exchanges, airports, banks, commercial premises, hotels, etc. The new towns are thus partly the consequence of the demand for bigger bureaucracies, and more African labour to man the building industry. Moreover, the growing body of European officials, traders and technicians, and their families, seeking to reproduce the pattern of European life in Africa, and the developing African middle class (with their tendency to imitate European consumption habits), generate new demands for semi-luxury goods and services. The demand for more cars and cameras, cooked ham and chocolate éclairs, cafés, cinemas, chiropodists and circulating libraries, means an increase in specialised agencies to meet these demands. It means also a limited growth of secondary industries, manufacturing beer, squash, cigarettes, bread, biscuits, clothing, as well as a large expansion in the demand for that basic African commodity—'boys'.

The following Table gives an indication of the remarkable post-war rate of growth of some of the new towns. (Where round figures are given, these are estimates.)

been much more spectacular than that of the Westerners, whose numbers barely doubled during the same period). In Accra, according to the 1948 Census, about three-quarters of the population were born in either Accra or the Colony (southern Gold Coast)—the remainder coming mainly from Ashanti, the Northern Territories, Togoland or French Africa. In Kumasi, on the other hand, only 56 per cent were Ashantis. In Cotonou M. Lombard estimated that 80 per cent belonged to the neighbouring region of south Dahomey.(4) In his study of Poto-Poto (the largest and most cosmopolitan of Brazzaville's three African towns) M. Balandier found that only 10 per cent of the adult population were Brazzaville born; another 67 per cent had migrated from neighbouring parts of Moyen-Congo; the remaining 23 per cent were long-distance immigrants—from the north of Moyen-Congo, Gabon, Ubangui-Shari, Chad, the Belgian Congo, and even the West African coast.(5)

Traditional migration routes have naturally influenced this process of swelling the new towns. "The great masses of Africans," M. Paul Henry says, "prove themselves to be superbly unconcerned with the frontiers established by the European Powers."(6) The flow of the Mossi of Haute-Volta and the peoples of the *Boucle du Niger* south to the Gold Coast and the Ivory Coast; of the Banyarwanda east into Uganda; of northern Nigerian and French African Moslems along the *hajj* route to the Sudan(7)—these movements have produced a floating 'foreign' population, depending mainly on agricultural wage-labour, on cocoa farms or cotton plantations, for a livelihood—of whom some drift eventually to the towns, living for the most part in their separate communities, the *Zongos* of the southern Gold Coast. These immigrants from Africa's depressed areas find themselves in much the same position as the Irish in Lancashire and York-shire in the 1840s—living at standards below those of the African townsmen among whom they settle, liable to be used as cheap labour to keep down wages and break strikes.

The inclination to migrate and to become urbanised is, understandably, much stronger among some peoples than others. The Ibos of eastern Nigeria have established themselves as sizeable minorities in the towns of western and northern Nigeria and the Cameroons. In much the same way the Bamileke, in the French Cameroons, have increased their numbers in Douala much more rapidly than the Doualas themselves, and have come to dominate the trade of the town.(8) In Bangui, in French Equatorial Africa, there is an important and growing Bamileke colony.(9) The Kikuyu in Kenya, and the Nubians in the northern Sudan, are also examples of peoples who seem to adapt themselves rapidly to town life and town jobs. In all these four cases there is a clear connection between migration and land shortage. But this adaptability cannot be entirely explained in terms of economic pressures. It goes too with a general Westernising outlook: for "the Bateke, in spite of their proximity to Brazzaville and their poverty, systematically reject urban life; whereas among the Bacongo the social climate is favourable to the travels of the young, which are regarded as a source of profit to the family".(10)

Why do the young men go? This is a question on which the Poto-Poto survey, carried out by M. Balandier and his colleagues, throws a great deal of light.(11) Economic motives are naturally dominant: the need to earn wages —to pay the bride-price, meet tax-demands, help one's family out of difficulties, buy a bicycle or sewing-machine —is a recurrent theme. So is the idea of a career open to

talents: the possibilities which the town presents of becoming professionally qualified—working one's way up
from apprentice to master-mason, or from 'boy-chauffeur'
to lorry-owner. Sometimes the motive is more precise—as
in the case of X, born at Mecca of northern Nigerian
parents settled at Fort Lamy, who saw the Sara people of
Chad being recruited and taken south for the building
of the Congo-Ocean Railway, grasped the business opportunities which this migration offered, and installed himself in Brazzaville in 1929 to work as a tailor.(12)

These economic aims tend to be mixed up with motives
of a more personal kind. People move to the towns, or to
a larger town, partly to escape from a traditional environment which has become intolerable: the man exploited
by his family, or his wife's family—"à Bangui il y a trop
de famille; on me demande trop de choses". Orphans and
suspects; children of a first wife, and those who believe
themselves the victims of sorcery—for these the town
represents a means of liberation: "À Brazzaville on dort
bien, on mange bien; quand on va avec la femme d'un
autre, on n'a pas d'histoire avec le commandant, parce-
que à Brazzaville personne ne se mêle pas de ce qui ne le
regarde pas." The 'commandant méchant'—the trouble-
making District Officer—is a recurrent figure in the
story, symbolising the demands and constraints of European authority; so is the reactionary chief, upholding
tradition and custom, and thwarting the demands and
aspirations of the 'progressive' and 'dynamic' young men.
When, as during the last war, the pressure of authority—
to get labour for road-making or rubber collection—was
intensified, African peasants responded, as peasants every-
where else have responded, by running away to the towns.
To these must be added the various attractive influences:
the man installed in the town who sends for a relative—

to have company, or to put him to school; the European who moves from the bush and brings his 'boy' or his 'mama' (girl-friend) with him. For many young men, too, immersion in the town serves as a modern form of initiation rite: a youth cannot expect to win a girl's favours unless he can show the brand of the town upon him. These factors affect the selective process of migration, and thus the kind of society that emerges in the towns. Their new citizens have already, in many cases, tasted opposition to authority; are looking for the opportunity 'bien vivre et s'amuser'—'not only to live but to live well'.

'Bidonvilles', 'shanty-towns', are the terms most often used to describe the new towns of Africa. The words give some impression of the facts—vast areas of slum houses, huts and shacks, hurriedly thrown together out of planks, corrugated iron, petrol tins, sacking, and anything that came handy, to house a continually increasing immigrant population. This type of town is familiar in most of colonial Africa. Only the Sudanic towns—Bamako, Kano, Omdurman—though subject to the same kinds of pressure, have largely preserved the tradition of mud-brick architecture, and with it a certain dignity and style, even in their newly constructed quarters.(13) And the predominance of Islam, expressed in their mosques, gives them a unity that is lacking in the multi-religious towns farther south. Among the shanty-towns there is diversity. Towns like Medina—the main African quarter of Dakar —have been laid out on a geometrical criss-cross pattern of intersecting streets (however chaotic their later development), reflecting the colonial interest in order and discipline; whereas in towns like Lagos, Accra and Sekondi, huts and tenements, shops and offices, appear mixed inextricably in one great urban huddle. Poto-Poto, though geometrically planned like Medina and sub-

ject to increasing overcrowding, is organised on the basis
of compounds interspersed with palm trees, making possible a measure of privacy. Congo towns, such as Brazzaville, Leopoldville, Elisabethville—essentially European
fabrications as their names imply—are also typical
*agglomérations urbaines*, where Africans of many tribes
and languages live mixed up together in artificially
created quarters and new housing estates. Most West
African towns on the other hand have more of an organic
character, syntheses of villages (like London or Paris); in
which each village, though absorbed by the growing
town, preserves its identity—with its traditional chiefly
families performing a decorative role—and where the
fusion of peoples is less complete. Moreover, every
African town reflects in some degree the outlook of the
colonial Power. Contrast the quiet country-town atmosphere of Bathurst—"very sleepy, very English; not a café
in the silent town", as M. Dresch puts it—with the vitality
and night life of its neighbour, Dakar.(14)

Against this background of diversity there is one common characteristic that repeats itself throughout colonial
Africa—the division between the European and the
African town. True, this division varies in degree and in
rigidity. It is only in the Belgian Congo, and to the south,
that there is a legal demarcation between the *ville blanche*
and the *ville indigène*, and legal restrictions upon intercourse between the two.(15) In British and French West
Africa, the barrier is rather social and customary—associated with differences in jobs, living-standards and social
habits, as well as with two relatively recent phenomena
—the importation of European wives, and the popular-
isation of the myth of White superiority. But north of the
Congo segregation has never been complete. In fact
Ikoyi, the Lagos garden suburb, has been a White man's

town, just as Yaba has been a Black man's town. But there has always been the odd African judge or Government doctor who lived, ex officio, in the White man's town; just as there was the odd European missionary (or, in French Africa, the *petit-blanc*) who lived in the Black man's town. In British West Africa Africanisation (in the Churches and in commerce, as well as in the State) is gradually destroying the social basis of segregation; and in French Africa housing shortages have forced more Europeans to reside in African towns.(16) Elsewhere the barrier between the two towns is preserved and justified (by Europeans); while in South Africa it is Government policy to make it absolute. This general pattern—of an African town separate from, and economically and politically subordinate to, a European town, the two towns being closely linked in regard to their economies and administrative systems, but unbelievably remote in respect of their human relationships—has an obvious bearing on the genesis of African nationalism.

There is indeed nothing new in this idea of urban *apartheid*. According to El Bekri, writing in the eleventh century, it was applied by the pagan Ghana kings (black Soninke, ancestors of the modern Sarakolle) who compelled their Moslem subjects to live in a separate town, six miles from the royal capital.(17) In reintroducing the system into the new towns of twentieth-century Africa, the new European rulers were simply applying a concept with which they had already become familiar in nineteenth-century Europe—whereby the rich lived in Bayswater or Cheetham Hill, and the poor lived in Bethnal Green or Ancoats. In Africa, as in Europe, this system had the advantage that the rich could pass most of their lives without seeing how the poor lived. Moreover, it could be defended on the same principle—that the culture of the

Blacks (or the poor) was fundamentally different from the culture of the Whites (or the rich), and that it would make for the greatest happiness of the greatest number if there was the minimum of contact between the two cultures. Thus it could be—and is—argued that so-called Colour Bars are in reality only Culture Bars; and that when enough Africans learn to use water-closets, to prefer bridge to drumming, and scandal to sorcery, and show themselves in other respects to be civilised men, the Culture Bar will automatically wither away. This theory, plausible though it may be, does not affect the present situation; nor alter the fact that African towns house, for the present, two nations—not only in Disraeli's sense, a nation of the rich (or relatively rich) and a nation of the poor; but also in a special, colonial, sense, the nation of the White (or relatively White) and the nation of the Black. And the correlation between being Black and being poor, being White and being rich, is sufficiently close to stimulate in most African towns a spirit of African radicalism, which tends to identify the claims of the poor against the rich with the claims of the Black against the White: a spirit expressed in such poems as this by a young Senegalese, David Diop:

> "*Souffre, pauvre Nègre! ...*
> *Le fouet siffle*
> *Siffle sur ton dos de sueur et de sang*
> *Souffre, pauvre Nègre!*
> *Le jour est long*
> *Si long à porter l'ivoire blanc du Blanc ton Maître*
> *Souffre, pauvre Nègre!*
> *Tes enfants ont faim*
> *Faim et ta case est vide*
> *Vide de ta femme qui dort*

*Qui dort sur la couche seigneuriale.*
*Souffre, pauvre Nègre!*
*Nègre noir comme la Misère!*(18)

In describing the new towns of Africa in these dualistic terms I have ignored so far the third element, the foreign merchants, shopkeepers and money-lenders, whose "commercial activities lie above the petty trading of most African women on street corners . . . and below the large corporate operations of most European trading companies"(19): Lebanese and Syrians for the most part in West Africa; Indians, Pakistanis and Goans in East Africa; Portuguese and Greeks, among others, in Central Africa. These communities of middlemen, performing a necessary but unpopular function, tend to live apart in their own distinct quarters, or ghettoes. Another kind of ghetto exists in some of the larger towns of northern Nigeria—Kano above all—where *Sabon Garis* (a Hausa term, meaning 'new towns') have been built to house the southern Nigerian immigrants, who come north to work for European commercial firms and Government departments—a semi-privileged class of clerks and accountants, foremen and teachers. This further breaking down of townspeople into physically separate communities—different in social origin, language, economic standards and mode of life—living often several miles apart, each largely confined within its own world, is inevitably a factor making for communal conflict.

For the African immigrant arriving in one of the new towns there are two pressing problems—to find a home and a job. Unless he is lucky enough to have a relative in whose house or compound he can install himself, a lodging may be hard to find. A series of counts in a small area of Sekondi in 1949 showed an average of 200 people sleeping in the streets or under open verandahs (hence the term 'verandah-boys'—used, in the same pejorative sense as 'paupers' in nineteenth-century England, to describe Dr. Nkrumah's political followers). Dr. Busia's description of housing conditions in the same area of Sekondi would apply to almost any of the larger African towns. The following is a sample:

"Sixteen rooms, 52 occupants. No kitchen, two bathrooms, one latrine. Rents, 10s. to 20s. The occupants cooked in the yard, some of them quite close to their living-rooms. Three rooms meant for kitchens had been converted into living-rooms and let at 10s. a month each. One room with a floor space of $9\frac{3}{4}$ feet by 7 feet was occupied by a man, his two wives, and three children, and stored with all their belongings and their food."[20]

With acute overcrowding go the usual concomitants— high rents, the failure of the public services, lack of sanitation, dirt and disease; a few public pit latrines, too dirty often to use, serving large communities; at rare intervals, maybe, a public water-tap. In Treichville, the main African quarter of Abidjan, the rent for a single room in a house of old planks is 10s. to 12s. per month; in a house of mud-brick, £1; in a house of brick or concrete, 30s. to £2—where an unskilled worker's monthly wage is roughly £5.[21] With the construction of new housing estates, often several miles distant from the centre of the town, the situation is slowly changing: above all in the Belgian Congo, where the *Office des Villes Indigènes* has been building 5,500 new houses a year in Leopoldville alone—but, since the population of the town is increasing at the rate of about 30,000 a year, pressure on accommodation continues.

The two problems—a home and a job—are often

closely linked, since it is normal for a new arrival to
pledge his wages in advance to pay the rent of a room, or
part of a room. Jobs are also hard to find: partly because
African peasants, like other peasants, lack any kind of
qualification that is useful in a town; partly because most
African towns have already expanded well beyond their
capacity to provide employment, and contain a pool
(averaging 10 to 15 per cent) of unemployed labour—
including a proportion of ex-schoolboys. With crude unemployment goes a great deal of disguised unemployment
—*parasitisme:* reflected partly in the quantity of Africans
who find their way into 'commerce', whose profit margins
on a small turnover help to raise the African cost of
living.(5)(12) Those described as 'washermen', 'public
writers' and 'bicycle-repairers' are often in fact parasitic
on the productive section of the African community; and
in Poto-Poto the description of 'fisherman' may sometimes be a useful cover for following the occupation of
pimp. (There are, of course, plenty of parasitic lines of
business among the European community too.) Another
characteristic of the rudimentary economy of the new
towns is the precariousness of jobs. M. Balandier gives an
example of one first-generation Brazzavillian, who started
as a *petit-boy* (the lowest grade of domestic servant), and
later became, successively, a general labourer, a mason, a
washerman, an apprentice tailor, and a restaurant pro-
prietor.(22)

The economy of the inflated town depends also upon
the institution which MM. Balandier and Sautter call
'parasitisme familiale'. In its mildest form this means no
more than the prolonged visit which relatives from the
bush—like Mr. Collins—pay their town cousin. In a more
developed form it involves the transformation of relatives
into dependants, who settle—like Penelope's suitors—in

the townsman's compound, and live at his expense. Dr. Busia gives figures from Sekondi to show how "the number of dependants increases with rises in salary: so that, while married men in the lowest income group (£2 to £4 per month) have on the average only 4.4 dependants, those in the highest income group (£15 to £25 per month) have 8.25". Hence "men earning comparatively high wages are often in financial difficulties".(20) This form of parasitism has its roots in the traditions of the extended family; and, though resented by the enterprising young, and regarded as an obstacle to individual advancement, respect for tradition, and unwillingness to break the ties that bind a townsman to his village and his people, help to preserve the institution. The relationship has moreover, in one sense, social utility, in that it serves as a rough-and-ready method of redistributing African incomes in favour of the poorest. And it is seldom that the victim does not receive some services—help in the house and suchlike—from those whom he supports.(12)

The new towns generate a social life of their own—unlike any life that has existed in Africa hitherto: deriving its special qualities, first from the new emphasis upon money and consumption; second from the search for liberty; and third from the influence of the European world and its values.

The larger African towns, though relatively feeble as centres of production, are organised with far greater efficiency from the standpoint of consumption. There is little that cannot be bought—by those with money to buy.(5) There is the whole range of durable consumers' goods, which help to determine a man's social status in the new hierarchy of the towns—bicycles, sewing-machines, gramophones, wireless sets, soft furnishings, and, for a small upper stratum, motor cars. There is edu-

cation which, even where it is formally free, involves out-
lay—and is another important determinant of social
status. There are places of enjoyment—bars, cafés, dance-
halls, cinemas. There is the customary heavy expenditure
on marriages and funerals (Dr. Busia gives £87 12s. as
typical expenditure by a Sekondi widow on the funeral of
a literate husband).(20) There are the various ways in
which life can be made a little easier—by gifts to those in
a position to issue permits and licences, or influence the
order of names on waiting-lists for houses or hospital
beds.(23) This combination of a spectacular increase in
the possibilities of consumption—as compared with village life—and an essentially low-wage economy leads
naturally to an effort to increase incomes by all available
means: individually, through petty trade, business side-
lines, prostitution, corruption, indebtedness (usurers in
Brazzaville charge interest-rates of 25 to 30 per cent per
month); or collectively, through trade-union pressure
and strikes.

Writing of early nineteenth-century England Mr. and
Mrs. Hammond described how the "changes that destroy
the life of custom . . . bring into men's minds the dreaded
questions which have been sleeping beneath the surface
of habit".(24) In contemporary African towns most
aspects of social life are affected in one way or another by
this questioning process: for example, the traditional
authority of the old. These towns are predominantly
young men's towns. In the quarter of Poto-Poto studied
by M. Balandier the average age was 25, and two-thirds of
the population were under 30. He quotes the remark of a
Brazzavillian: "Life here is too hard for the old: it's best
for them to go home to the village."(5) The notion of the
right of the young to live their own lives and enjoy their
economic independence unhampered by their elders, has

spread from the great towns to the small towns within
their areas of influence. M. Mercier has recorded some of
the popular songs of the young men of Djougou (a town
of 5,000 inhabitants in north Dahomey) who go to
Kumasi for work:

> *"Mon père m'a dit: paresseux!*
> *Mais avec quelle recolte a-t-il payé l'impôt?*
> *Avec la recolte de mon travail.*
> *S'il m'insulte encore, j'irai à Ketao.*
> *Là je trouverai un camion pour Kumasi,*
> *Et je gagnerai de l'argent pour moi!"*(25)

With the questioning of parental authority goes a questioning of the traditional forms of marriage. The songs of
Djougou glorify romantic love, and the amorous successes
of the young—themes which the older men regard as
immoral. In Cotonou, partly because of the inflated
bride-price, 'trial marriage' is becoming increasingly
popular, particularly among young Catholics.(4)
Eighteen out of 50 Cotonou residents questioned by M.
Lombard approved of this arrangement. This is linked
with the fact that in the towns, where there is normally
keen competition for scarce women, women also have become aware of new possibilities of liberty. The women of
Poto-Poto have "a clear understanding of their market
value". The *femmes libres* of French and Belgian Africa,
living in their own establishments, entertaining whom
they please, are able to enjoy a standard of comfort and
a freedom from work that few wives can hope for. This
revolt against authority is expressed also in the field of
religion: through the growth of new Christian heresies
(discussed in a later chapter); of the Ahmadiyya movement (a heterodox revivalist form of Islam); of the syncretistic Tigare cult in the Gold Coast;(20) and, at least

among the educated minority, of scepticism and free thought. In the 1950 Census 295 Lagosians are listed as 'Freethinkers' (including 20 Freethinkers under the age of four), and 3,142 as 'Agnostics'. In Bangui, a much less cosmopolitan centre than Lagos, M. Lebeuf speaks of the growing influence of 'idées laïques'.(9) This is the kind of intellectual climate in which Kwame Nkrumah's slogan —"Seek ye first the political Kingdom"—is readily acceptable.

It is misleading to describe African townsmen as 'de-tribalised' or 'Europeanised', for in many respects tribal and kinship ties remain strong; and cultural borrowing does not prevent the town African from remaining essentially African. But, inevitably, close and regular contact with Europeans affects African town life at every point. Food habits change: Africans eat bread, made from imported flour, rather than manioc, yam or cassava. Men wear shorts and shirts, and, more gradually, women substitute frocks for cloths. (In Johannesburg "the young African woman's taste in dress compares on almost even terms with that of the European woman".(26)) Women acquire European domestic arts—knitting, sewing, washing with detergents, ironing, baby care—the use of powdered milk, layettes and chamber-pots. Traditional forms of dance are modified, or abandoned for Western styles (though here it is American and West Indian influences that are dominant). Devotion to football has become passionate and universal: when Accra plays Lagos, or Leopoldville plays Douala, this has the ritual importance of a feast of the Church. European magical techniques for achieving success and warding off ill-fortune tend to take the place of traditional magic—aspirins, Horlicks, correspondence courses, diplomas—and African entrepreneurs set up agencies to sell these essential commodi-

ties. Values approved by the European bourgeois—
individual achievement, self-help, efficient organisation,
the ornamental function of wives—and his symbols of
social standing—whisky and large cars—tend to be taken
over by the new African middle class. The depth to
which these European modes of living have penetrated
varies, of course, a great deal, both from class to class and
from town to town. They have naturally gone much
deeper in old centres of European influence, like Dakar
or Freetown, than in newer centres, like Kano or Fort-
Lamy; and farther in a territory like the Belgian Congo,
where the principle is to 'civilise', than in a territory like
northern Nigeria, where the principle has been to preserve traditional social institutions. Moreover, with the
development of self-conscious nationalism, employing
such methods as the boycott of European goods, the European cultural revolution has begun to be opposed by an
African cultural counter-revolution.(27)

The resemblances between the new towns of modern
Africa and the new towns of early nineteenth-century
England are neither superficial nor accidental—resemblances in regard both to the physical environment and
mode of living. A large proportion of African townsmen
—like our forefathers—live in overcrowded shacks, or
rooms in lodging-houses, for which they pay an exorbitant
rent out of low earnings. They queue for latrines, where
these exist, and their wives queue for water. Most of them
are unskilled 'hands', who move from job to job, with
periods of unemployment. To economise on food many
live on one main meal a day. Most are first-generation
townsmen, who remain peasants at heart—still in touch
with their villages, and dreaming of returning 'home'
when they are old and prosperous.(28) It is against this
background that the often-discussed problems of African

town life—drink, gambling, prostitution, crime and delinquency—have to be understood. These were also the problems of the towns of early nineteenth-century England. The spectacular increase in the consumption of imported alcohol—nine-fold in French West, and twenty-fold in French Equatorial Africa, as compared with pre-war—can be paralleled by what Brougham described as the "frightful increase in the consumption of ardent spirits" in the England of the 1830s.(24) The 'pilot-boys' of Sekondi-Takoradi, who live by piloting seamen to the homes of prostitutes, receiving 8s. out of every £1 a prostitute makes—who work in gangs within which "there is intense loyalty and confraternity";(20) the *Sanje Kulele* of Elisabethville (a Swahili word meaning 'colour-changers', since courtesans change their frocks several times a day);(29) the proliferation of casinos, beer-houses and brothels; the comparative frequency of crimes of violence and crimes against property—these are familiar by-products of the new urban world. In describing drink and prostitution as "two of the main scourges of modern Africa" (with the cinema as a third), M. Jean Malonga, senator for Moyen-Congo, was misjudging the African social situation as many of the founders of the early Temperance Societies misjudged the British. In fact these are symptoms only, which "follow with inevitable necessity out of the position of a class left to itself, with no means of making fitting use of freedom".(3) Where such means do, in some degree, exist, African townsmen have already begun to show their capacity to create a new indigenous civilisation—as qualitatively distinct from European civilisation as the African town is physically separate from the European town. Some of the characteristic institutions of this new civilisation form the theme of the remainder of this book.

# 2

## THE NEW ASSOCIATIONS

THE effect of the new towns is to split men into separate self-seeking atoms. But since, as Hume pointed out, sympathy and benevolence are natural human passions, African townsmen find a variety of ways of linking themselves together again. This linking process, on a basis other than simple kinship, is helped partly by the sheer size and diversity of town populations; partly by the existence of physical centres (less essential than in cold climates—but desirable none the less), where men and women, with particular interests in common, can collide with one another: churches and chapels, schools, halls, clubs, bars, shops, cinemas. The exuberant growth of associations in African towns is a point which has often been noticed.(1) Less attention has been given to the contribution which, in varying degrees, these associations have made to the development of national movements. First, they have made it possible for Africans to recover, within the new urban context, the sense of common purpose which in traditional African society was normally enjoyed through tribal organisations. Second, they have given an important minority valuable experience of modern forms of administration—the keeping of minutes and accounts, the handling of records and correspondence, the techniques of propaganda and diplomacy. In this way they have made it possible for the new urban leadership to acquire a kind of informal professional training—rather in the way that Nonconformist and working-class associations trained the new Labour leadership in nineteenth-century Britain. Third, in periods of political ferment and crisis, these associations provide the cells around which a nation-wide political organisation can be constructed.

What types of association? Rigorous classification on a functional basis is impossible, since there are no clearly defined limits to the activities that any association may choose to undertake. Functions are dependent upon the common interests of members, and there may be many points at which these interests intersect. An association brought into being to meet a particular recognised need may develop other activities in the course of its history: a lorry-drivers' union may decide to run literacy classes; a football club may formulate proposals for constitutional reform. All African associations are concerned, to some degree, to provide outlets for the African genius for sociability—through *tam-tams*, dances, feasts, picnics and the like. Many attempt to compensate for the weakening of the traditional system of social security by protecting their members against the normal human emergencies— operating as Friendly Societies and Burial Clubs.(2) Moreover, in a colonial society hardly any association can be totally disinterested in current political questions— though the extent of its interest is likely to vary with the historical and local situation. And where civil liberties are restricted or non-existent—as in Belgian Africa— political questions tend naturally to be discussed, and claims asserted, through overtly non-political organisations, *évolués*' clubs and Christian youth groups. This diffusion of African civic consciousness—its tendency to express itself through many-sided, multi-purpose organisations—can be illustrated by one or two examples.

Tribal Associations are essentially organisations of a

new type. They are not a survival from pre-European society. They exist to some degree throughout colonial Africa, though they are particularly proliferous and flourishing in southern Nigeria. "In the Eastern Provinces there are, in the words of one official Report, 'Improvement Unions, Improvement Leagues, Welfare Leagues, Community Leagues, Tribal Unions, Patriotic Unions and Progressive Unions too numerous to mention'."(3) Whatever name they go by, these associations have the common characteristic that they are based upon traditional social groupings—the lineage, clan, village-group or tribe. But they are normally led by the educated younger men. They have developed, for the most part, over the last twenty years, and have been concerned with two main purposes—to provide a channel for 'progressive' public opinion at home, and to maintain an organised link between the 'sons at home' and the 'sons abroad'. Mr. Ottenberg has described in detail how one such body, the Afikpo Town Welfare Association in eastern Nigeria, has concerned itself, since its foundation in 1950, with a campaign against female nudity, the settlement of disputes within the village-group, the provision of scholarships to the local secondary school, 'send-offs' and receptions for members visiting England—and, generally, has acted as a pressure-group to stimulate local improvements.(4) The importance of these associations, or their 'foreign' branches, in the social life of the new towns is obvious. They provide the easiest and most natural basis of association for new immigrants, and ease the process of transition from village or small-town to urban life. In Bangui it is normal for a new arrival in the town to visit the local head of his 'nation' (unless he has been in serious trouble at home—in which case he will naturally wish to keep out of the way).(5) In Poto-Poto there were in 1950 twelve *Amicales*, organised on a tribal basis, with an average membership of about a hundred, predominantly clerks.(6) Most of them were mainly concerned with the preservation of tribal ties in a cosmopolitan, fragmented town, through regular Saturday and Sunday evening *tam-tams* in the compound of a senior tribesman. But one at least, the *Mbongi* of the Balali, was also involved in schemes for the modernisation of tribal custom.

There are three ways in which these Tribal Associations contribute to the development of African nationalism. They provide a network of communications, entirely under African control, through which ideas, information and directives can be diffused from the great towns to the bush. In the towns themselves they tend to foster, or keep alive, an interest in tribal songs and dances, history, language and moral beliefs; and thus, in part, to offset the Europeanising influences at work.(7) (They may at the same time help to stimulate a tribal form of nationalism. The links betwen the Ibo Union and the National Council of Nigeria and the Cameroons, and the much closer relationship between *Egbe Omo Oduduwa*—a Yoruba cultural society—and the Action Group, help to account for some of the characteristics of those parties.) Moreover, some Tribal Associations—the Ibibio Union in Calabar, for example—have played an active part in the education of an African élite, not only through providing scholarships for the children of tribesmen, but also through founding and managing their own independent schools.(3)

Clubs, particularly in British Africa, are a form of association which deserve more notice than they have received. Sports clubs—above all football clubs—are, of course, an unvarying element in the culture of African towns. The names of the football clubs of Sekondi-

Takoradi, listed by Dr. Busia, reflect the poetic imagination of their founders: *Heroes, XI Wise, Mighty Councillors, Mighty Poisons, Great Titanics, Simple Winners, Zongo Vipers, Rowlands, Western Wolves, Hearts of Oak, Hasaacas*.(2) (There are many reasons for the sociological importance of football in contemporary Africa—among them the fact that it provides one of the few inter-territorial meeting-points for Africans.) Of more immediate political interest have been the clubs of the African intelligentsia and professional class, such as the Rodger Club in Accra, the Hodson Club in Kumasi, the Island Club in Lagos—clubs with the tendency towards social exclusiveness that is familiar in the clubs of the British upper-middle class. These independently financed and managed African clubs, in provincial towns as well as capital cities, have served as centres, not only for relaxation and social intercourse—in symbolic opposition to the almost all-White European clubs—but also for the exchange of news and ideas and the framing of policies: a function which cannot equally well be carried out by the officially financed, supported and supervised *cercles culturels* of French and Belgian Africa.(8)

The Old Boys Association is another type of organisation which recurs throughout colonial Africa. Often its functions are, as in Britain, predominantly social—running football teams and holding periodic reunions. But sometimes it spreads over into other fields. The Old Achimotan Association in the Gold Coast, for example, in the period immediately following the Second World War, took the initiative in organising and conducting evening classes for Kumasi workers. The *Association des Anciens Elèves du Lycée Terrasson de Fougères* at

Bamako was instrumental in bringing into being the first trade unions in the French Sudan in 1937. It was in the Technical School Old Boys' Club at Atbara that the Workers' Affairs Association was born in 1946; and the WAA was the precursor of the modern Sudanese trade-union movement.(9) Youth Associations have shown a similar tendency to extend their field of operations. In the early post-war years the Ashanti Youth Association (AYA) canalised much of the opposition of Ashanti 'young men' both to chiefly authority and to colonial rule; later it became one of the main supports of the Convention People's Party in Ashanti; in 1955, with self-government almost an accomplished fact, it transferred its allegiance to the National Liberation Movement and the idea of Ashanti autonomy. In French Togoland *Jeunesse Togolaise* (*JUVENTO*) has played a leading part in the movement for Togoland unification and independence.(10) On a smaller scale, M. Holas has carried out an admirable case study of *La Goumbé* (the word is derived from the name of a local dance)—a Moslem, and predominantly Dioula, youth organisation, for both sexes, in Treichville, Abidjan.(11) *La Goumbé* combines the functions of emancipating young women from family influences; assisting the process of matrimonial selection; providing, on a contributory basis, marriage and maternity benefits (including perfume and layettes for the newborn); preserving the Dioula tribal spirit; running an orchestra; and acting as the local propaganda agency for the *Rassemblement Démocratique Africain* (the dominant political party in the Ivory Coast): it even maintains its own police force.

The importance of women's associations naturally varies in relation to such factors as the position of women and women's societies in the traditional system; the local influence of Christianity and Islam; the extent to which women take part in the economic activities of the town—as traders, nurses, teachers, etc. (One interesting consequence of the appearance of the new class of *femmes libres* has been the development of Courtesans' Unions to protect their interests. In Poto-Poto, for example, there are women's associations with exotic names— *Rose, Lolita, Diamant, Étoile, Brillant*—which act as Friendly Societies, provide their members with lavish funerals, organise socials and outings, and maintain the rate for the job).(6) In non-Moslem areas—and even, to a smaller extent, in Moslem areas—the growth of women's social consciousness has been an essential aspect of the process of nationalist awakening. This has been particularly marked in southern Nigeria, where, as early as 1929, the Aba Riots were the result of the initiative and direction of women's organisations;(12) and where, during the post-war period, Women's Unions have developed vigorously. Some are conducted as co-operatives: "there are women's societies which run a bakery, a laundry, a weaving workshop, a calabash manufactory, a gari mill, and so on. In these ways the women provide themselves with necessary services, cut out the middleman, and raise their own standard of living."(13) One of the most interesting of these—the Egba Women's Union in Abeokuta, inspired by that remarkable woman, Mrs. Funmilayo Ransome-Kuti, claims a membership of 80,000 women, paying subscriptions of 1s. a year; operates as a weaving co-operative; runs a maternity and child-welfare clinic; and conducts literacy classes for illiterate women. It has also taken an active part in local politics, and was chiefly responsible for the agitation that led to the abdica-

tion of the Alake of Abeokuta in 1948.(14) This tendency
to move over into political activities is common among
women's organisations also—as in Uganda, where specifically Christian associations, such as the Mothers' Union
and YWCA, played a large part in the popular agitation
for the return of the Kabaka of Buganda; one by-product
of which was the creation of an explicitly political
women's organisation—the Uganda African Women's
Congress.

It may be argued that these associations are many of
them unstable and short-lived; their aims confused or
utopian; their financial basis precarious; their methods
sometimes brutal, sometimes ineffective; their discipline
feeble; their philosophy incoherent; their leaders frequently corrupt, self-seeking, ignorant, irresponsible, and
at war with one another. Precisely the same criticisms
were levelled against the popular organisations thrown up
by the new towns of early nineteenth-century England.
Their importance, however, lies partly in their rich
variety, reflecting the range of interests and aspirations
of the Africans who created them; partly in the evidence
they provide that African vitality—far from being
crushed by the squalid surroundings and crude discipline
of these colonial towns—has been stirred to new forms of
expression. The associations of contemporary Africa are
democratic, not in the sense that they can serve as models
of democratic organisation; but in the older sense, that
they have been constructed by a *demos* which is slowly
discovering, by trial and error, the institutions which it
requires in order to live humanly and sociably in the
urban world into which it has been thrust. Essentially
they are an outcome of the "discontent excited by the
philosophy of life of which the new town [is] the symbol

and expression".(15) For this reason, if for no other, they deserve careful examination. In the next three chapters I propose to examine in more detail three main types of association which have been especially involved in the growth of nationalism—separatist churches and prophetic movements, trade unions, and political parties.

# 3

## PROPHETS AND PRIESTS

At this point it would be desirable to discuss the contribution of religious organisations and beliefs of all types to the development of African nationalism. In fact it will only be possible to deal with a limited sector of the field—the Christian separatist Churches and prophet movements. One reason for choosing this theme is that these are bodies which have depended almost entirely upon African initiative and direction. But undoubtedly European or American-controlled Missions—Catholic, Anglican and Nonconformist—have also played an important part in stimulating national consciousness; and there are questions relating to their contribution which it would be interesting to pursue farther. To what extent, for example, have the catechists, Sunday School teachers and local preachers, whom the Missions have trained, found their way into positions of leadership within the various national movements? In what precise ways have Mission schools, and particularly the secondary schools, influenced the thought and practice of the Africans whom they have taught? How far have any of the Mission Churches in the various territories become so far 'Africanised', in their outlook as well as in their hierarchies, that they have come to be regarded as national institutions?[1]

Equally, the extent to which Islam has tended to assist, or check, the rise of nationalism in the various regions in which it is a force, demands closer study. The links which

Islam provides, particularly through the *hajj*, with Asian peoples and ideas; its capacity to transcend colonial frontiers; its freedom from racialism, and from political associations with imperial Europe—such factors enable Islam to appeal in a special way to Africans in this period of national awakening. On the other hand the effectiveness of Islam as a stimulus is limited by the conservatism of its orthodox spiritual leaders, and by the formalism of traditional Koranic education. Here the most interesting questions are probably those which relate to the character, outlook and strength of the opposition to traditionalism in Islam, as expressed in Mahdist movements, as well as in the penetration, particularly in French Africa, of Wahabist and modernist doctrines, through such channels as the teaching and propaganda of former students of Al-Azhar University.(2) In Moslem, as in Christian, Africa, religious dissent and political radicalism are often closely related. A third theme would be the influence of traditional Animist beliefs and institutions, e.g. ancestor cults and secret societies, and of pagan revivalist movements—such as Tigare in the Gold Coast, Muvungi in the southern Belgian Congo, and (in one of its aspects, according to Dr. Leakey) Mau Mau in Kenya —in the shaping of African nationalism.(3) In concentrating in this chapter on the new heresies of Christian Africa I do not mean to suggest that these other topics are unimportant.

The tradition whereby Christian institutions and symbols serve as a form through which men can express their aspirations for social and political change is as ancient as the Church itself. Since the Donatist revolt in fourth-century North Africa a succession of Christian sects have combined separatism (in effect, if not in intention) in matters of Church organisation with demands for social justice, stated in the language of religion.(4) It is understandable that, in the conditions of twentieth-century Africa, the sense of oppression by colonial authority, and the moral crisis accompanying the disruption of tribal society and the invasion of commercial values, should have combined to produce movements of the same separatist type within the African Churches. In what circumstances have these dissenting movements established themselves? How far has religious dissent served as an outlet for the expression of nationalist claims?

The first question can be answered fairly simply. For the peoples of pre-European Africa, as for other pre-capitalist societies, religious belief normally included a metaphysic, a cosmology, and a moral and political theory.(5) The language of politics was at the same time the language of religion. Thus it is natural that any movement which has sought to arouse the mass of Africans, still for the most part religious in their modes of thinking, to a new conception of their rights and duties should use religious symbolism for this purpose. Hence in some regions, such as the Moyen-Congo, the dissident sects have shown themselves more effective in their appeal than the political parties;(6) for the language of the sects is itself an unsophisticated and familiar language. And where a high proportion of the adult population is illiterate, the use of symbols, images and ceremonial counts for more. Even in the Gold Coast, with its much higher level of economic and educational development, the effort of the Convention People's Party to build up a mass political movement involved the use of religious rituals —the singing of 'Lead, Kindly Light', the reciting of nationalist prayers, and a Creed in which Kwame Nkrumah took the place of Christ and Sir Charles Arden-Clarke was substituted for Pontius Pilate.

For popular discontent to express itself through specifically Christian symbols, it is necessary for Christian Churches to have been established for some time, and for evangelisation to have made substantial progress, so that the symbols have already become, for many Africans, familiar and acceptable. A measure of saturation must have taken place. Thus a second reason why religious dissent appears as a recurrent theme in the history of African nationalism is the fact that, throughout most of Africa, the Missions were established well in advance of the period of European political penetration. Christian beliefs, traditions and language were the first elements of European culture which Africans had the opportunity to absorb. For African Christians (Protestants in particular) the Bible became common ground, the essential book of reference, much as it had been among the sects of seventeenth-century England. Dr. Roland Oliver describes how, at the end of 1893, on the eve of the British Government's ratification of the Uganda Protectorate, a vigorous revivalist movement developed among the Baganda:

"Scenes occurred which put one in mind of Gregory Nazienzen's description of Constantinople on the eve of the Arian controversy. The missionaries were constantly being stopped as they walked about the streets by people racing out of their houses with books in their hands to ask the meaning of obscure passages. What was a winepress? How far was it from Jerusalem to Jericho? In what did the wealth of Capernaum consist? The embarrassed clergymen had to write home to headquarters for reference books and commentaries."(7)

Although this particular religious revival was in no sense anti-European (and the Native Anglican Church in Uganda has, in general, been peculiarly successful in keeping revivalist movements within the Church), much subsequent political unrest among the Baganda has expressed itself in Christian formulae: the 1949 disturbances and the Kabaka conflict are recent examples.

A third factor in the situation has been the evident relevance of the Jewish-Christian tradition to the situation of colonial Africa. For Africans who have become conscious of the pressures of colonial rule, the theme of an oppressed people that is also a chosen people, now wandering in the wilderness, but destined to find a leader drawn from its own ranks who, under divine guidance, will bring it to the promised land, has an immediate and obvious appeal. The identification of British, French or Belgians, with Egyptians, Philistines or Romans, and of one's own African community with the children of Israel or with the early Christians, is natural and inevitable. The interpretation of the conflict between European rulers and subject Africans as a conflict between technical and military power and a moral idea, in which the eventual triumph of the idea is historically necessary, seems implied in the whole Jewish-Christian approach to history. Dr. Sundkler describes how some of the independent Bantu Churches in the Union of South Africa have developed the doctrine of the 'reversed colour-bar' in Heaven. Heaven is for Black men only. "Shembe (founder of the Nazarite Church) at the gate turns away the Whites, because they, as the rich men, have already received their good things, and he opens the gate only to his faithful followers." Parables can be given the same kind of esoteric African meaning. "There were ten virgins. And five of them were White, and five were Black. The five Whites were foolish, but the five Blacks were wise; they had oil in their lamps. . . ."(8) The persecution of the Saints of the early Church can be paralleled by the persecutions of African prophets. Professor Buell's account of the capture

and trial, by a Belgian military court, of the Congolese
Prophet, Simon Kimbangu, in 1921, reads very like an
early Christian document:

"At the trial Kimbangu and his followers defended themselves in a dignified manner. Questioned as to why he thought
he was a prophet, Kimbangu quoted a verse to the effect that
'thou hast hid these things from the wise and prudent, and
hast revealed them unto babes'. When the President of the
court asked what 'these things' were, Kimbangu replied by
repeating the ten commandments. When he started to repeat
the seventh he was ordered to stop by the captain, whose
native concubine was present in the court room."(9)

It is indeed so understandable that Africans should see
themselves in the heroic role in the Christian drama, if
once they are permitted to read and enjoy it, that the
Portuguese have shown consistency in restricting the en-
try of Protestant Missions into Portuguese Africa, on the
ground that they are the advance-guard of African
nationalism. "To tell a person he is able to interpret the
Bible freely is to insinuate in him an undue autonomy
and turn him into a rebel. . . . A Protestant native is
already disposed towards—not to say an active agent in—
the revolt against civilising peoples."(10)

At this stage it will be as well to see how far a distinction can usefully be drawn between what I have called
'separatist Churches' and 'Prophet movements'. Dr.
Sundkler, whose *Bantu Prophets in South Africa* is much
the most thorough study of African dissenting movements that has yet appeared, distinguishes between
'Ethiopian' and 'Zionist' Churches in the Union.
Churches of the 'Ethiopian' type (so called because 'Ethiopia' symbolises independence of European control) are
self-governing Bantu Churches, which have either

seceded from European-controlled Mission Churches—usually on the issue of Church government—or seceded from the original breakaways. While emphasising the principle of African control (with episcopal authority often modelled closely on chiefly authority), "their church organisation and Bible interpretation are largely copied from the patterns of the Protestant Mission Churches from which they have seceded". Churches of the 'Zionist' type, on the other hand, are those which use terms such as 'Zion', 'Apostolic', 'Pentecostal', 'Faith', to describe themselves. Their organisation is looser and more unstable. They tend to centre upon a particular prophet (who may claim to be in direct telephonic communication with the Holy Ghost). They stress spontaneity and emotionalism in their rituals—confessions, dreams, healing, drumming and dancing, sacred dress, speaking with tongues, purification, divining, ceremonial visits to High Places. Women play a large part in their activities. They are hostile to European techniques of education and medicine. They are syncretistic, in the sense that they carry over into their doctrines and worship values and rituals derived from traditional religion. M. Balandier has suggested that the 'Ethiopian' Churches, more 'aristocratic and modernist', to some degree correspond with the early stages of nationalist claims; while the 'Zionist' Churches, more 'popular and confused', correspond with the later, more radical, nationalist reaction.(6) The distinction between the two types is, at any rate, important. Separatist 'Ethiopian' Churches are interesting—from the standpoint of a study of nationalism—chiefly because they involve the assertion, within the framework of the Church, of the claim for African self-government. The interest of the 'Zionist' Churches, on the other hand, lies in the fact that they are associated with the personality of a particular prophet, and derive much of their force and appeal from the apocalyptic hopes of a total reconstruction of society which he inspires.

Why have the separatist Churches seceded? While there is no single explanation of 'Ethiopianism', certain common factors seem to recur in different African territories. One, not necessarily the most important, has been the desire to restore tribal unity, in opposition to what are felt to be the disintegrating influences of the various European Missions. The first of the separatist Churches in South Africa, the Tembu Church, was formed in 1884 by Nehemiah Tile, a Wesleyan minister, and a Tembu nationalist, who wished "to adapt the message of the Church to the heritage of the Tembu tribe. As the Queen of England was the head of the English Church, so the Paramount Chief of the Tembu should be the *summus episcopus* of the new religious organisation."(8) The same idea—of a tribal Church with its own tribal Apostolic Delegate—survives among some of the peoples of the Belgian Congo who have been subject mainly to Catholic evangelisation. The principle of 'Africa for the Africans' in opposition to the authority of European hierarchies has played a large part in almost all secessions. The oldest of the Nigerian separatist Churches, the United Native African Church, was founded in 1891, partly as a protest by a group of Nigerians against CMS criticisms of Bishop Crowther, the first African Anglican Bishop. "Resolved that a purely Native African Church be founded for the evangelisation and amelioration of our race, to be governed by Africans."(11) The view that the Mission Churches, with the extra-territorial companies and the Administration, are simply three aspects of a single Imperial fact, is—or has been—widespread throughout colonial Africa. The following extract from a leaflet by Charles Domingo, a Nyasaland separatist Church leader, in 1910, quoted by Mr. George Shepperson, puts poetically a universal separatist attitude:

"The three combined bodies, Missionaries, Government, and Companies, or gainers of money, do form the same rule to look upon the native with mockery eyes. It sometimes startles us to see that the three combined bodies are from Europe, and along with them there is a title, 'CHRISTENDOM'. . . . If we had power enough to communicate ourselves to Europe we would advise them not to call themselves 'Christendom' but 'Europeandom'. Therefore the life of the three combined bodies is altogether too cheaty, too thefty, too mockery. . . ."(12)

External influences have played a part, though not as a rule a preponderant part, in stimulating separatism. In its early days the South African 'Ethiopian' movement certainly owed a good deal to the influence of Negro Churches—particularly the African Methodist Episcopal Church (founded in Philadelphia in 1816).(13) By 1906 at least 150 Africans from the Union had gone to America to study, "some of them with definite Ethiopian connections". But there was also an African reaction against colonisation by American Negro missionaries, who were believed to spend money collected in Africa "on purely American interests, and not on Ethiopic interests".(8) Probably the most important single outside stimulus was the American-born Garvey movement, in which the strands of Ethiopianism and Pan-Africanism were closely interwoven. Marcus Garvey—a Jamaican negro who in 1914 founded the Universal Negro Improvement Association, described himself as 'Provisional President of Africa', created African orders of nobility, established an

African Orthodox Church, published the *Negro World*, and organised international conventions for Africans and non-African Negroes—was successful in spreading the idea of independent African Churches as an instrument of African liberation. The impact of 'Garveyism' can be traced in British and French West Africa and the Cameroons, as well as in South Africa, particularly during the period of unrest and revolt that immediately followed the First World War.(14)

Another American-based agency which has promoted the growth of religious dissent is the Watchtower Movement (the missionary arm of Jehovah's Witnesses), preaching Pastor Russell's doctrine of the 'millennial dawn'. The Watchtower seems first to have appeared in Nyasaland in 1906–7, introduced by Mr. Joseph Booth, originally a Baptist missionary from Melbourne, a wandering radical "in search of the absolute".(12) Nyasaland, Northern Rhodesia and Katanga (where it is known as *Kitawala* and officially banned) have traditionally been the main Watchtower strongholds, though the influence of the movement has since spread to other parts of Africa. The importance of the Watchtower, as of other American sectarian missions—Seventh Day Adventists and the various Baptist Pentecostal sects—lies mainly in the fact that they have made Africans familiar with "more fundamentalist, egalitarian interpretations of the Scriptures, as well as providing new avenues for separatism".(15) In a situation in which Africans were already schismatically inclined, they have widened the field of choice.

Dr. Parrinder, in his account of the independent Churches of Ibadan, has pointed out the error of supposing that polygamy has been a primary cause of separatism. He gives one example of a Nigerian Church which broke away on this issue—the United African Methodist ('Fishmonger') Church, founded in Lagos in 1917 in reply to a monogamy campaign launched by the Chairman of the Methodist Mission. A number of leading Methodists were found to be polygamous, deprived of office, and made to sit at the rear of the church: they and their supporters, claiming that the "Church was not European, but African", then seceded. But, in general, while polygamy tends to be more tolerantly regarded in independent than in Mission Churches, this is essentially one aspect of the broader separatist principle—that Christian ethics, as commonly understood in western Europe, must be adapted to the African tradition and social setting; and those elements in Mission teaching which derive primarily from European custom discarded. As a Nigerian pamphleteer, somewhat naïvely, argued: "In England [polygamy] is regarded as an offence against the State. I dare suggest reasons for this. The English woman is very jealous of love and does not like to share her husband's love with another. Our women are not like this. . . ."(16) Monogamy is thus frequently regarded not as a Christian, but a European, institution, lacking scriptural sanction—a view with which Dr. Leakey would seem to be in sympathy.

Separatism, or 'Ethiopianism', it might then be argued, represents the restatement, in terms appropriate to twentieth-century Africa, of certain basic Protestant principles: the appeal from Authority to the Scriptures; the emphasis on the right of individual interpretation; the protest against rigidity in moral and social theory; the demand for a national Church and a national hierarchy. And, though Catholic Missions have bred their own separatist Churches and leaders, it is natural that Protestantism should be the more fruitful source of new protest movements.

What part have the separatist Churches played in the development of African nationalism? Outside the Union of South Africa these Churches have not yet been studied with sufficient thoroughness for more than a tentative answer to be given. Historically, separatism has sometimes been associated with political radicalism and sometimes with quietism. One example of an independent Church with a strong radical flavour was the United Native Church in the French Cameroons (an offshoot of the English Baptists), under the leadership of Lotin Samé, in the period of political ferment after the First World War. "During 1922–3 the whole town of Douala seethed with this religious 'revolt' in which natives paraded up and down the streets singing anti-European hymns."(9) Similarly in Nyasaland, on the eve of the First World War, Mr. Shepperson speaks of the 'little Church communities' associated with John Chilembwe (who later led the 1915 Shire Highlands Rising), Charles Domingo and Joseph Booth, acting as 'the main avenues of agitation'; and adds that "perhaps the most important element in Chilembwe's nationalism was the conception he may have had of the role which a national Church can play in the creation of national feeling".(12) And in the most recent period the National Church of Nigeria and the Cameroons—with its prayers to the God of Africa, its hymns to freedom and its Litany beseeching deliverance from imperialism—has functioned as a kind of ecclesiastical instrument of radical nationalism in eastern Nigeria.

However, in most of contemporary Africa, the essential point of the separatist Church is rather—as M. Balandier has argued—to transfer to the spiritual and ecclesiastical plane opposition to European authority in general, and to make possible, on this plane, the reconstruction of

African communities under African leadership: a process which is particularly liable to occur under an authoritarian colonial system, where religion is "the only field within which emancipation is possible".(6) Hence the proliferation of independent Churches of all types (over 800, with more than three-quarters of a million adherents) in the Union of South Africa, where a highly authoritarian régime increasingly blocks all other roads by which Africans might seek their emancipation. Hence, too, their apparently declining importance, as an outlet for social and political aspirations at least, in British and French West Africa, where since the war political parties, trade unions and the like, have offered more promising techniques for solving the problems of African subordination and poverty. Dr. Sundkler describes the Bantu independent Church in South Africa as "one of the few psychological safety-valves . . . in a society of racial discrimination directed against the African"—a view borne out by a study of one particular South African Church, the Church of Christ, conducted by Mr. Mqotsi and Mr. Mkele.(17) Its spiritual and temporal head, Bishop Limba, is a great chief and political manager, who enjoys great wealth (including De Soto and Chrysler cars), much of which he uses on behalf of the community. The community on their side can feel that they enjoy vicariously the power, wealth and prestige of their leader. Bishop Limba is addressed as ' father', and the members of the community call one another 'brother' and 'sister', thus creating a new solidarity replacing tribal ties. It is, say the authors, 'a very dignified community', within which a Puritan ethic is practised: drink and self-indulgence are forbidden, and girls are expected to live a chaste life. "Many look upon the Church as the key to salvation from the oppressive laws imposed by the White

man, and from exploitation. This is made clear by the
fact that a great deal of emphasis is laid upon material
strength; and business enterprise, as a means to independence, is encouraged." Thus within the closed circuit
of the Church it is possible to develop the self-governing
society that it is forbidden to construct outside.

The term 'safety-valve' is suggestive. There seems certainly some resemblance between the appeal of 'Ethiopianism' to Africans whose social life has been disintegr-
ated by colonial rule, and the appeal of Methodism to
the working class of early nineteenth-century England,
faced with the disintegrating force of the Industrial Revolution. Both movements have offered a 'connexion',
within which brotherly relations can be restored; human
dignity can be rediscovered; men and women of ability
can attain to positions of leadership and power; those excluded, on the ground of class or race, from national history can, within a setting of their own choice, make their
own history: in which hymns and prayer-meetings and
preaching can produce a sense of exaltation, and release
from the squalor and oppression of the new towns; enjoyment of happiness in Heaven is assured, and—for some at
least—enjoyment of prosperity on earth becomes a possibility. Both movements have canalised a sentiment of revolt, but, in matters outside the control of the Church,
have tended to direct it towards quietism.

The dividing line between 'Ethiopian' and 'Zionist'
Churches is admittedly not a sharp one. The former may
model themselves closely on their parent Mission
Churches, or they may develop marked 'Zionist' characteristics. But the broad distinction between priest and
prophet, between founding a Church and inspiring a popular movement, between the separatist and the messianic
ideas, between dissent and enthusiasm, seems reasonably

clear—even though the priest, like John Wesley, may have prophetic qualities, and the prophet, like George Fox, may leave a Church behind him.

There is a remarkable consistency in the pattern of the prophetic movements that have occurred in regions of Africa exposed to Christian influence—a pattern which reproduces many of the features of such movements throughout the history of the Universal Church.(18) The prophet receives his divine call in a dream or vision. In the case of Isaiah Shembe, the best known of the Zulu prophets, "his first revelation was imparted to him when as a young boy he was praying in the cattle-kraal. During a thunderstorm the Word was brought to him by lightning; 'Cease from immorality (*ukuhlobonga*)'". William Wade Harris, the Liberian prophet, who is said to have baptised 120,000 people in the Ivory Coast in 1914–15, received his 'call' from the Archangel Gabriel, who appeared to him in a vision. Simon Kimbangu, a carpenter and Protestant catechist from Thysville in the Belgian Congo, was "touched by the grace of God on the 18th March, 1921", and directed to go out and heal the sick. Donisio, an illiterate Catholic from the Kenya-Uganda border, dreamed that he saw Christ with two Africans, one of whom was wearing medals. Later he met the prophet Elijah Masinde, who had formerly been a noted footballer, and still wore his football medals; Donisio recognised him as the prophet whom it had been revealed that he should follow.

The prophet then enters upon his ministry—often after a period of severe internal conflict. The ministry takes, as a rule, the form of a campaign against idolatry, the burning of fetishes, healing, casting out demons, miracle-working, baptism of the faithful, withdrawal to high places. The Puritan element in the prophet's mes-

sage is usually fundamental—the condemnation of forni-
cation, theft and lying. The prophet acquires special
titles which express his special sanctity and powers.
Shembe was 'the Promised One', 'the Liberator'; Kimbangu had twelve names, corresponding to the twelve
months of the year—'the Prophet', 'the Holy One', 'the
Saviour', 'the Chief', 'the Flag', 'the Ladder to climb to
Heaven', 'the Gate of Heaven', 'the Ship which carries
the Soul', 'the Way of the Soul', 'the River', 'the Priest'.
The prophet may even be regarded by his followers as the
Black Christ, who has displaced the pale Christ of the
Missions. "Jesus came first as a White man. But now he
has come as a Black man, in the flesh, through Shembe."

Up to this point the prophet movement, although
naturally incurring the disapproval of the Missions—
since it distorts their doctrines and empties their churches
—does not necessarily come into conflict with the colonial
administration. Its outlook may not be anti-colonial or
anti-European. The prophet may even, like Harris in the
Ivory Coast, preach submission to secular authority. It is
principally the millenary aspects of the doctrine, and
their implications, that tend to produce a clash between
prophetic power and colonial power. The prophet an-
nounces that 'these things are coming to an end'—that the
present corrupt social order will be replaced by a *Reg-
num Dei*. The early followers of Kimbangui believed
that the world would end on October 21st, 1921, when
fire from Heaven would wipe out the White men. "Other
Kimbanguist preachers were reported to have declared
that the American Negro would come and deliver his
Congo brother from White oppression, and that the
second coming of Christ, for the same purpose, was im-
minent." (9)

The Watchtower movement clearly owes much of its influence to its millenary outlook. Its claim that the world, as we know it, would end in October 1914 contributed to revolt in Nyasaland. In contemporary Africa the argument that "we are living in a time of unparalleled woes" provides an empirical basis for the central Watchtower doctrines: "(a) the Kingdom is at hand in this generation; (b) only Witnesses will be accepted into the Kingdom; (c) life in the Kingdom is earthly and not spiritual; (d) in the Kingdom there will be a complete absence of all the ills of this world . . . and all women will have children."

Belief in the inevitable doom of this world usually implies contempt for the civil authorities of this world. In one Kimbanguist village in Moyen-Congo the villagers told the chief: "Toi, tu n'as qu'à te taire, ce n'est pas l'Administrateur qui donne la grace. Il ne faut pas obéir à l'Administrateur, il faut obéir à Dieu." From this attitude springs the refusal to co-operate in Government-provided services, which colonial authorities have regarded as a peculiarly unenlightened characteristic of prophet movements. *Dini Ya Misambwa*, Elijah Masinde's sect, disapproved of maternity centres on the ground that they gave African women medicines to prevent them from bearing children; of Mission schools; and of soil conservation. The principle can be extended to cover rejection of everything of European origin. Mr. Kenyatta has described how members of the Kikuyu sect, *Watu wa Mngu* (People of God) "have burnt foreign articles and thrown away all utensils which are of foreign origin, on the ground that they are ritually unclean". This form of prophetic xenophobia can give rise to a variety of fantasies—such as the belief that the bullets of

European rifles will turn to drops of water when confronted with the faithful—a comforting but dangerous doctrine.

In the tradition of the Old Testament and the Puritan sects, the Prophet's community is an Elect, a people apart. Its sense of separateness from the world is symbolised in a variety of ways—in sacred dress, for example. White robes are normal among the 'Zionist' communities of South Africa, though other special colours may be revealed in dreams. The Kakists in Moyen-Congo—a sect founded by the prophet Simon Mpadi in 1941, in the Kimbanguist tradition—were so called because during their religious ceremonies the faithful were obliged to wear a khaki uniform—a sign of 'deliverance and victory'. Sometimes the growth of beards is also a sign of separateness. Believers withdraw into caves and holes in the ground for purposes of meditation. They experience possession and 'shaking': the *Watu wa Mngu* "in their prayer . . . hold up their arms to the sky facing Mount Kenya; and in this position . . . they imitate the cries of wild beasts of prey, such as lion or leopard, and at the same time they tremble violently. The trembling, they say, is the sign of the Holy Ghost, *Roho Motheru*, entering in them".

The best organised of the sects have their special hymn-books, in which the idea that "Christ Jesus died sufficiently for all men, . . . but primarily, really, and effectually for none but the Elect",(19) is clearly brought out: as in this dance hymn from the Nazarite hymnbook:

> *"I shall dance, I have hope*
> *I am a Nazarite girl.*
> *I do not fear anything,*
> *Because I am perfect."*

Or in this, more militant, hymn from the Kimbanguist *Chants du Ciel*:

*"Jésus, Sauveur pour les Élus et Sauveur pour nous tous.*
*Nous serons les vainqueurs envoyés par Toi.*
*Le Royaume est à nous. Nous l'avons.*
*Eux, les Blancs, ne l'ont plus."*

It is understandable that, even where prophet movements do not attempt to act on their conviction that the rule of Europeans must soon give way to the rule of Saints, colonial Governments which tend to regard every expression of popular feeling as 'subversive' should see in such movements a potential danger to the régime. In this they are only behaving as the civil authorities in first-century Judæa or in seventeenth-century England behaved when confronted with a similar problem. Hence, south and east of the Congo, experience of official repression has tended to strengthen the nationalistic aspects of the prophet movements. The sects can appeal to a history of persecutions and martyrs to support the justice of their cause. Mwana Lesa (meaning 'Son of God'), who introduced *Kitawala* into the Belgian Congo, was hanged in Rhodesia in 1926. Simon Kimbangu, who was sentenced to death in 1921, had his sentence commuted to life imprisonment and died in gaol in Elisabethville in 1950. André Matswa, more of a politician than a prophet in his lifetime, from whom the Moyen-Congo Matswanist heresy derives, was deported to Chad in 1930 and eventually died in prison in 1942. Simon Mpadi escaped four times from prison. Mulomozi wa Yezu ('God's Deputy') and Alleluia, *Kitawala* leaders, were hanged in 1944 for their part in the Bakumu revolt, in the Stanleyville district of the Belgian Congo. There were 3,818 political prisoners (of whom 631 were 'declared dangerous'), mainly connected with one or other of the prophetic sects, in the Belgian Congo in 1952; and over the preceding years the number had been gradually increasing. Ideas of martyrdom and resurrection are naturally associated. Matswanists "refuse to believe that Matswa is really dead; or accept the fact as merely provisional, awaiting the second coming of the prophet whom some call 'Jesus Matswa'." In Brazzaville they even spoil their ballot papers at election time by inscribing the name of André Matswa.

There is an obvious parallel between the Messianic beliefs of these Christian-influenced prophet movements and the Mahdist tradition within Islam, according to which "the Last Day would be heralded by a period of confusion and oppression brought to an end by the appearance of one called the Mahdi (the God-guided one). The chiliastic kingdom of the Mahdi would then be destroyed by the Dajjāl (Anti-Christ), but the Prophet Isa would return, kill the Dajjāl, and fill the earth with justice by ruling according to the Law of Islam."(20) In Moslem Africa south of the Sahara, apart from the great Mahdi, Muhammad Ahmad the Donqolāwi, in the 1880s, there have been numerous lesser Mahdis during the period of colonial rule, e.g. in Senegal, the French Sudan, and Adamawa (in the Cameroons).(21) In northern Cameroons an interesting variant of Mahdism occurs, according to which the Mahdi has already come and gone, and this is now the epoch of government by the Dajjāl; the necessary preliminaries for the end of the world are already taking place, and it will in fact come about 1,400 years after the death of the Prophet. The connection of Messianism and Mahdism with periods of history which are felt to be periods of oppression, social upheaval and frustration, has often been noted. Quite apart from the internal stresses generated by the European impact, it would be wrong to underestimate the sensitiveness of the mass of Africans, Moslem, Christian and Animist, to the two World Wars in which they have been involved, and the rumours of a third. The special humiliations which are imposed upon Africans in colour-bar countries, and the difficulty of conceiving how this situation can be transformed gradually, by human agents, naturally encourages belief in a transformation which will be supernatural and cataclysmic. Moreover, the crests of the prophetic waves in the French and the Belgian Congo have tended to coincide with the troughs of economic depression. "The three periods of serious conflict coincided with the three periods of economic crisis— 1921–2, with the collapse of prices of colonial products (which provide the only important source of money incomes); 1930–1, with the shock of general depression; and after 1940, during the years of poverty and rising prices."(6)

The contribution of these movements to the development of African nationalism has clearly been much more important in Bantu Africa than in West Africa; and within Bantu Africa it has varied from region to region. Their main achievement, in their areas and periods of greatest strength, has undoubtedly been to diffuse certain new and fruitful ideas, in however confused a form, among the African mass, the peasants in the countryside and the semi-proletarianised peasants in the towns, for the most part: the idea of the historical importance of Africans; of an alternative to total submission to European power; of social ties that are based upon common beliefs and purposes rather than upon kinship; of a community in which women enjoy equal rights and duties with men. These ideas have been widely accepted among the adherents of prophet movements, partly because they were intrinsically acceptable, but partly also because they have been propagated by men who were themselves of the mass, not of the new urbanised educated élite: a carpenter like Kimbangu; an ex-soldier like Matswa; a Salvation Army catechist like Mpadi: literate, but accustomed to use their literacy mainly for Bible reading, from which source their ideas were chiefly drawn. It is true that these movements represent a relatively primitive phase in the development of nationalism, in which political and social reconstruction is envisaged simply as a new world order, and rejection of European authority is expressed through the characteristic forms of 'enthusiasm'. But at least the prophets have awakened men's minds to the fact that change can occur; and the ablest of them, like their European prototypes, have shown themselves wholly capable of constructing a myth, a literature and an organisation.

nationalism. With the growth of a market economy, increasing economic differentiation is taking place throughout colonial Africa; illustrated by the situation in the cocoa-producing areas of western Nigeria and the Gold Coast, where there is now an influential class of larger farmers, substantial employers of labour, with their motor cars, town houses and comfortable standards of living.(1) It is this new middle class—traders, contractors, transport owners, professional and administrative workers, as well as farmers—which has so far tended to dominate the emerging national movements. It is from their ranks that the African members of the Legislative Assemblies of British West Africa and the Sudan, and of the Territorial Assemblies of French Africa, are principally drawn. African business (particularly timber) interests played an important part in the founding of the United Gold Coast Convention in 1947. There has been an evident connection between African transport, commercial and banking interests, in eastern Nigeria especially, and the National Council of Nigeria and the Cameroons. In the Belgian Congo the early manifestations of national consciousness have been associated with the growth, since the Second World War, of a new class of prosperous business men, chiefly in Leopoldville. In two cases at least farmers' organisations have been prominent in nationalist activity and agitation: M. Houphouet's *Syndicat Agricole Africain* in the Ivory Coast,(2) and Mr. Musazi's Uganda African Farmers' Union.(3) In European circles it is sometimes regarded as a sign of 'ingratitude' that the section of the African community which has gained most from European-stimulated economic development should develop this 'anti-European' attitude. In fact the African middle class, following the example of its predecessors in other parts of the world, has reached, or is moving towards, a stage at which it has both the resources and the confidence to challenge the economic and political predominance of foreigners, both European and Asian.

In this chapter, however, I propose to discuss the claims of a different economic group—wage and salary earners —and its typical form of organisation—the trade union: partly for the practical reason that there is rather more material available; partly because of the intrinsic importance of trade unions in the history of almost every modern nationalism.

Who are the African workers? The terms 'worker' and 'wage-earner' mean something so different in contemporary Europe and contemporary Africa that any discussion of African trade unionism must begin with some general remarks about the African labour situation.

The extremely low level of industrialisation in colonial Africa implies a relatively small labour force in relation to the total population, and a concentration of that force in agriculture (mainly of the plantation or settler-managed type), mining, transport, commerce and the public services. There has so far been very little development of factory industry, outside Southern Rhodesia and the Belgian Congo and a few great towns like Dakar. No precise statistics of the size of the wage- and salary-earning population exist for many African territories. The following Table does not claim to give more than a rough approximation to the facts. (For convenience, an estimate of the number of trade unionists in each territory is included in the Table, where figures are available.)(4)

## TABLE II

| Territory | Number of Wage-earners | Percentage of Total Population | Number of Trade Unionists |
|---|---|---|---|
| French West Africa . . | 350,000 | 2.0 | 70,000 |
| French Equatorial Africa | 190,000 | 4.2 | 10,000 |
| French Cameroons . . | 125,000 | 4.0 | 35,000 |
| Nigeria (and British Cameroons) . . | 500,000 | 1.5 | 150,000 |
| Gold Coast . . . | 200,000 | 4.5 | 25,000 |
| Sierra Leone . . . | 80,000 | 4.0 | 20,000 |
| Gambia . . . . | 5,000 | 2.5 | 1,500 |
| Belgian Congo (and Ruanda-Urundi) . | 1,000,000 | 8.5 | 6,000 |
| Uganda . . . . | 280,000 | 4.0 | 1,500 |
| Kenya . . . . | 450,000 | 8.0 | 32,000 |
| Tanganyika . . . | 400,000 | 6.0 | 400 |
| British Somaliland . . | 2,000 | 0.3 | nil |
| Somalia . . . . | 25,000 | 2.0 | 3,700 |
| Zanzibar . . . | 5,000 | 4.0 | 900 |
| Northern Rhodesia . | 250,000 | 13.0 | 50,000 |
| Nyasaland . . . | 120,000 | 5.0 | 1,000 |
| Southern Rhodesia . | 530,000 | 24.0 | nil |
| Sudan . . . . | 200,000 | 2.0 | 100,000 |

These figures suggest that there are perhaps between four and five million wage-earners in colonial Africa. If the Portuguese territories (for which no reliable estimate is available) are taken into account, the higher figure would seem the more probable. But this figure does not, of course, refer to 'workers' in the European sense of the term—those, that is, who (except during periods of unemployment) are wholly and continuously dependent upon wages or salaries for a livelihood. Many African workers are in fact still peasants, not entirely detached from their villages or from traditional agriculture, becoming wage-earners intermittently, spasmodically, or seasonally. The process of 'proletarianisation' extends far beyond the body of wage-earners employed at any given moment.(5) But, while wage-earners represent a relatively small proportion of the total population of colonial Africa—about 5 per cent—and stable, regular wage-earners a much smaller proportion, this does not mean that their influence on the course of events is likely to be negligible. In China in 1940 there were only two million industrial workers.

The situation of the African worker has thus to be understood against the background of a rudimentary capitalist economy. One characteristic of this economy is its dependence upon migrant labour.(6) Agriculture forestry and mining in particular, in the more developed regions—e.g. the coastal fringe of West Africa, the Gezira in the Sudan, the Rhodesian Copper Belt—draw a large part of their labour from adjacent, or distant, more depressed colonial territories. And migrant workers are, in general, resistant to trade-union organisation. Even those industries, like transport, which normally depend primarily upon locally recruited labour, often have a very high labour turnover. For example, in 1947, among the African employees of the Kenya and Uganda Railway, only 16.9 per cent had more than ten years' service; almost 50 per cent had less than three years', and 30.2 per cent less than one year's service.(7) In Atbara, on the other hand, the chief railway centre of the Sudan, the presence of an exceptionally stable body of workers seems to have contributed to the development of a remarkably vigorous trade-union movement.(8)

In mining and plantations especially, there is a tendency to regard a labour force as comparable with a military force, to be housed in barracks and kept under semi-military discipline. Writing of Southern Rhodesia, Mr.

Boris Gussman says: "The conception of African urban life, as expressed not only in its architecture but also in the legislation that controls it, is that of providing boxes for machines or stables for draught beasts."(9) Even where, as in the Belgian Congo, there has been a serious effort to substitute decent houses for barracks and tin shanties, the policy of providing a separate 'location', under management control, for mining workers, railway workers, etc., still survives.

The familiar characteristics of low-wage economies throughout the world are to be found in colonial Africa. Low wages are justified on the ground that African labour is 'inefficient', and inefficiency is itself in large part the consequence of the existing levels of earnings. On the Kenya and Uganda Railway "the inability of the African to obtain meals when natural hunger occurs is a serious factor in his inefficiency".(7) Even where, as in the Belgian Congo or on the Copper Belt, the provision of rations by employers may ensure a more satisfactory diet, the system tends to be resented by African workers in the same way, and for the same reasons, as truck in this country. Two other factors have operated to focus the attention of African workers on the wage question during the period since the Second World War. One has been the inflationary situation, which has meant that a good deal of trade-union energy has necessarily gone into the effort to maintain or improve real wages in the face of a rising cost of living. The other has been the increasing employment of Europeans in areas of industrial expansion—such as the Belgian Congo, the French Cameroons, Uganda, the Rhodesias—and with it a growing awareness of the great disparity between European and African earnings. In Southern Rhodesia, for example, the average earnings of a European worker amounted in 1952 to £595, and of an African worker to £56 10s. In Northern Rhodesia "the value of the minimum European remuneration in the copper-mining industry exceeds, by approximately 500 per cent, the value of the present maximum remuneration of the highest-paid African surface worker".(10) One consequence of this disparity is that African trade unions, when confronted by the official argument that the national economy cannot bear a general wage increase, are apt to reply that the cost of such an increase could be met by cutting down expenditure on salaries and emoluments for the expatriate staff.

Low wages are correlated, in part, with lack of specialised skill. The ratio of unskilled workers—*manoeuvres sans spécialité*—to skilled and semi-skilled—*ouvriers qualifiés*—in the towns of French Africa seems to work out at about three to one.(11) Again, it is reasonable to correlate the relatively advanced level of trade-union organisation in such centres as Atbara and Dakar, with the concentration there of relatively large numbers of skilled and semi-skilled workers. The difficulty of organising unskilled African workers is increased by the fact that most of them are illiterate and that most industrial towns (except in the Sudan) are polyglot, though there is a growing tendency for a local vernacular to be accepted as a workers' lingua franca—Wolof in Dakar, Bambara in Bamako, Yoruba in Lagos. Thus workers' movements are confronted with more complex problems of communication in contemporary Africa than in early nineteenth-century England.

Like the English town labourer of the 1830s, the African worker, if he wishes to be accepted into the new economy, has himself to accept the new industrial discipline. He has to give up the relative freedom which he enjoyed as a farmer or craftsman, implying that he 'worked extremely hard when the occasion demanded'—but these periods of intensive effort were related to seasonal needs, tribal obligations and supernatural sanctions—and submit to an external authority, imposing European conceptions of continuous effort, punctuality and maximum output. Work becomes dissociated from familiar rhythms, rituals and symbols. It becomes an affair of fines, deductions and sometimes thrashings. The mouthpiece of authority is often "a low-salaried European or 'coloured' member of the staff whose chief qualifications for the post are a harsh manner and a ready flow of invective in the native tongue".(9) One of the African's answers to this new discipline is absenteeism—like the Sheffield journeymen of 1792, whose practice it was said to be "to work for three days in which they earn sufficient to enable them to drink and riot for the rest of the week".(12)

Perhaps the most constant factor in the African industrial situation is the division between White employers and managers and Black workers. This situation is by no means confined to recognisably colour-bar countries. Those who are trained as engineers in France have difficulty in finding employment in French West Africa, on account of the unwillingness of most directors of firms to appoint Africans to posts in which they will be in a position to give orders to Europeans.(13) Even in that Black Man's Country, Liberia, Firestone, the great rubber company, is entirely managed by its American senior staff, who have created their own little White Man's World, with all its exclusiveness and colonial tabus. Of most of Africa it is true that "there is almost no meeting-point for the two classes except at work".(14) Differences between the situations in different territories turn largely on the point at which the African's progress is blocked.(15)

In the Rhodesian Copper Belt Africans are stopped from becoming skilled workers. In the Belgian Congo they are prevented from becoming managers or technologists. In British West Africa there is now, in principle, a career open to talents—except as regards the higher management of mines and commercial firms. The fact that, in both State and large-scale private enterprise, it is normally the European who plays the part of employer, while the African is in the role of worker, makes it inevitable that trade unions, where they are allowed to exist, should serve partly as vehicles for nationalist demands.

The guiding principle of large-scale enterprise in Africa is Paternalism, which Professor Brady regards as the appropriate theory of 'feudalistic capitalism'.(16) Harmony between management and workers is conceived as depending on a system of welfare, which is "logically 'totalitarian'—that is, it attempts to control both form and content of the *totality* of worker ideas and activities." The worker does not merely live in the company's location and receive the company's rations; he also sends his children to the company's schools; is treated in the company's hospital; spends his leisure seeing the company's films, playing football for the company's teams, praying in the company's church or chapel, and (if he is literate) reading the company's news bulletin. Independent trade unions fit ill with this conception, since they are liable to disturb business harmony. 'Feudalistic capitalism' prefers Works Councils (*Conseils d'Enterprise* in the Belgian Congo), which can be managed from above.

The situation is not, of course, static. The provision of technical education is being expanded and improved—both through technical colleges and schools and through special training courses, such as those run by the *Centres de Formation Professionelle Rapide* in French Africa.(17) Some of the great mining companies, above all the Belgian *Union Minière du Haut-Katanga*, in addition to providing their own very efficient systems of training for African technicians, have largely succeeded in substituting a stable for a migrant labour force—so that today half the *Union Minière's* 20,000 employees have ten years or more of service.(18) There is an increasing body of second, and even third, generation African townsmen, with a tradition of skill and a pride in the fact that they are workers. For all that, African trade unions are essentially the product of a primitive type of industrial society; and their problems, aims and tactics have to be understood in this historical context.

Before the Second World War trade unions scarcely existed in colonial Africa. Indeed, industrial, legal and political conditions scarcely permitted their existence. Western, Creole, influence seems to have led to an earlier development of trade unionism in Sierra Leone than elsewhere: an African Railway Workers' Union was in existence in the 1920s;(19) and as far back as 1874 the *Illustrated London News* published a picture of a Negro strike in Freetown. In the Union of South Africa the wave of strikes in 1919–20, particularly the successful strike of the Cape Town dockers and railwaymen, brought the Industrial and Commercial Workers' Union (ICU) into being, which bore the essential marks and suffered the eventual fate of the early nineteenth-century 'One Big Union'.(20) In French Africa the first legal African unions were created in 1937, as a result of the granting by the French Popular Front Government of limited rights of trade-union organisation—withdrawn again under the Vichy régime. In general, where workers' organisations

existed, they were often little more than *ad hoc* strike
committees, operating in a semi-underground, conspira-
torial fashion. The sporadic strikes which occurred in
British and French Africa in the 1920s and 1930s—the
Thiès-Niger Railway strike of 1925, the Sierra Leone
Railway strikes of 1919 and 1926, the strike on the
Northern Rhodesian Copper Belt in 1935—resembled
the 'turn-outs' in Britain before the repeal of the Combination Acts, in that they were regarded, and handled,
as illegal, and, if sufficiently serious, as 'rebellions'.
(The 1926 Sierra Leone Railway strike was described by
the Governor, Sir Arthur Slater, as "a revolt against
Government by its own servants".) And, like the 'turn-
outs', they involved occasional acts of violence and
sabotage.(21)

Thus the development of trade unionism is a characteristic of the most recent, post-war, phase of African history.
It is a development which has been virtually confined to
British and French Africa, since it is only there that independent trade unions have enjoyed a legal existence.
The situation in the Belgian Congo is complex. In
theory, trade unions have been legal since 1946. In practice, the fact that the local Belgian administrator has the
right to attend all union meetings has effectively re-
strained trade-union development, though recently the
Socialist and Christian Federations, which cater principally for European workers, have begun to organise small
numbers of Africans. (22) In British Africa the process
of granting legal recognition was a gradual one, in part
the consequence of war-time pressures, and the influence
of the British Labour movement within and upon the
war-time Government. The degree to which unions in
fact secured effective recognition, or continued to operate
on the borderland between legality and illegality, varied

from territory to territory. Administrations differed, and still differ, in their attitudes to such important matters as the conditions under which legal strikes can take place, the right of Government employees to take part in strikes, sympathetic strikes, the right to picket, the use of trade-union funds for political purposes, and so forth. But, broadly speaking, except in Southern Rhodesia, the principle laid down in the Gold Coast Trade Union Ordinance, 1941, that "the purposes of any trade union shall not by reason merely that they are in restraint of trade be unlawful", is now accepted.(23) In French Africa the right to associate, to strike, and to take part in the collective fixing of conditions of work, was secured in 1946, and written into the Constitution of the Fourth Republic. These rights were confirmed, elaborated and extended in the 1952 *Code du Travail d'Outre-Mer*. (24)

It is often argued that trade unions are an exotic growth in modern Africa, fostered by Governments of the Left in post-war Britain and France. The evidence does not support this view. It suggests rather that the tendency of African wage earners to form combinations "for the purpose of maintaining or improving the conditions of their working lives" was operating in British and French Africa well before trade unionism began to receive encouragement and help from the metropolitan countries—during the period indeed when it was still discouraged and suspect. Major Orde-Browne, who studied the labour situation in British West Africa in 1940, speaks of the appearance of 'nascent' or 'embryo' trade unionism in Nigeria, the Gold Coast and Sierra Leone:

"The objects and scope of trade unionism are not fully understood, and many of the fallacies and misconceptions characteristic of the first half of the nineteenth century undergo a curious resurrection. Quite inappropriate purposes are contemplated as, for instance, the group who were anxious to form a trade union of Mohammedans. The line of demarcation between the activities of a trade union and those of bodies such as friendly societies, insurance companies or political organisations is not understood."(25)

This official comment gives an indication of the spontaneity of African trade unionism—the natural tendency of those who promoted the first unions to regard them as multi-purpose organisations, which should attempt to meet the whole range of the workers' needs, rather than seek to copy contemporary Western European models. (Craft guilds, which have developed among independent artisans in 'modern' trades—goldsmiths, carpenters, tailors, barbers, shoemakers, bicycle-repairers, etc.—taking over many of the functions of the traditional lineage meeting, appear to have this same many-sided character. "To make merriment with each other in joy and to sympathise with those in sorrow" is one of the aims of the Iwo Carpenters' Union in Western Nigeria.)(26) The Workers' Affairs Association, the first Sudanese trade union—founded in 1946, when trade unions were still illegal organisations—included in its original list of aims a wide range of functions, over and above the improvement of its members' living standards: mutual help in times of illness, death and unemployment; the establishment of saving schemes and co-operative societies; the organisation of 'literary and scientific lectures'.(8) The fact that these aims have been imperfectly realised is subsidiary. What is interesting is that the move to set up trade unions in the Sudan arose, apparently without external prompting, out of a consciousness among workers of needs—and not only economic needs—which the existing industrial system failed to satisfy. The Sudan is a particularly clear illustration of the general point—that the

effect of legal recognition of African trade unions was to
remove a major obstacle in the way of combination, not
to create the idea.

It is however also true that, during the past ten years,
the development of African unions has been influenced
in a variety of ways from outside: through the appointment of specialist Trade Union Officers by the British
Colonial Office,(27) and the establishment in French
Africa of the *Inspection du Travail*; through the assistance of metropolitan trade-union bodies—CGT, CFTC
and *Force Ouvrière* in the case of French Africa, the
TUC (and also certain individual unions, like the
National Union of Mineworkers) in British Africa;
through the encouragement and propaganda of international trade-union centres, the World Federation of
Trade Unions and (latterly, in British Africa) the International Confederation of Free Trade Unions. Whether,
or how much, African trade unions have on balance bene-
fited from these external influences is a question which
cannot at this stage be answered. One unfortunate effect
has certainly been to import into Africa divisions within
the European trade-union movement. From the standpoint of African trade unionists, Trade Union Officers
(with individual exceptions) are often regarded as agents
of the colonial Government, whose chief concern is to
maintain industrial peace, discourage strikes and foster
unions of an amenable, non-aggressive type. At the same
time contact between the leaders of African and metropolitan trade unions, through reciprocal visits, missions,
conferences, special courses of training and observation,
has certainly helped African trade unionists to gain an
insight into techniques of organisation, bargaining and
negotiating. This is particularly true in the case of the
leaders of the CGT and CFTC unions in French Africa,

whose relations with their parent bodies in France have been a good deal closer than the relations between the independent trade-union organisations in British Africa and the British TUC.

The difference in structure between the trade-union movements of British and French Africa has had far-reaching effects upon union development.(28) In French Africa, as in Algeria, the pattern of metropolitan trade unionism repeats itself. The CGT, CFTC and *Force Ouvrière* have established their own organisations and headquarters in French West and Equatorial Africa, Togoland and the Cameroons, to which individual unions are affiliated. The CGT was first in the field and is the strongest, from the point of view both of numbers and organisation, of the three centres, accounting for about two-thirds of the trade unionists in French West Africa. The CFTC's influence is limited to certain regions—Senegal, French Guinea, Dahomey, Yaoundé, Brazzaville. The *Force Ouvrière* is numerically weak, and includes a large proportion of European workers, who are under strong moral pressure not to associate with the CGT in French Africa, even though they may have been formerly CGT members in France. In addition to these three metropolitan groupings there are certain independent, non-affiliated unions, of which the most important is the French West African *Fédération des Cheminots Africains* (with a membership of about 15,000), which broke from the CGT after the great 1947 railway strike.

This French African form of trade-union organisation has had certain interesting consequences. First, it has not necessarily given rise to as much internal disunity as might appear: in French West Africa the CGT, CFTC, *Force Ouvrière* and independent *Cheminots,* have maintained a co-ordinating committee, which played an important part in the effort to secure the passing and implementation of the 1952 *Code du Travail*. Second, the African sections of the metropolitan confederations have in practice been largely autonomous, and their leaders have shown imagination in relating their policies to the actual demands of African workers. Thus CGT unions, though regarded by Europeans as Communist, are regarded by most Africans as 'African', and are often so described. The CFTC, though closely associated with, and fostered by, the Catholic Missions, has in fact a majority of Moslem members in French West Africa, and admits theists of all types (including Animists) to its affiliated unions. (The final 'C' stands for *Croyants*, not for *Chrétiens*.) Third, one effect of this system is to strengthen the central organisation—CGT, CFTC, or FO—as compared with the individual unions: this has obvious advantages from the standpoint of trade-union efficiency, at a stage when many individual unions are small, unstable and lacking in experience and leadership. Fourth, as in the sphere of politics, there is a marked tendency for the demands of French African trade unionists to be dominated by the idea of equality, in the sense of equality of wages and conditions and equality of trade-union rights for African and European workers. For example, the 1947 railway strike had as its objective the realisation of a *cadre unique*, which would include both African and European railway workers. The extreme importance attached by the French African trade unions to the 1952 *Code du Travail* was due primarily to the fact that its intention was to secure equality of rights for African workers in such matters as the forty-hour week, holidays with pay, and (partially) family allowances.

In British Africa and the Sudan, on the other hand,

where trade unions have developed on a territorial basis, with no permanent links between the various trade-union movements, the natural basis of organisation has been the individual union. Initially, unions have tended to spring up around the demands and grievances of small groups of workers, employed in a particular enterprise, or craft, or locality, or some combination of the three/ For example, the unions affiliated to the Nigerian Trade Union Congress in 1945 included the UAC Singlet Factory Workers' Union, Lagos; the CMS Bookshop African Staff Union, Lagos; and the Lagos and Ebute Metta Barbers' Union.(29) In 1952 two-thirds of the Gold Coast unions and over half of the Nigerian unions were listed as having less than 250 members. It has none the less been possible to build up a small number of fairly powerful well-organised unions on an industrial basis, particularly among mineworkers (Northern Rhodesia, Gold Coast), railway workers (Sudan, Nigeria, Gold Coast), public utility workers (Nigeria); and among sections of the salariat, such as teachers and local government officers (e.g. the Nigerian Union of Teachers and the Nigerian Federal Union of Native Administration Staffs).(30) In most British African territories there have also been efforts to develop a central organisation of a TUC type, which should be able to act as a 'General Staff' to the entire trade-union body, and deal on its behalf with the territorial Government. In general these central organisations have flourished only during periods of crisis—the 1945 general strike in Nigeria, the 1950 general strike in the Gold Coast—and shown signs of disintegration at other times, as a consequence of personal rivalries, disagreements over questions of strategy and tactics, administrative pressures and WFTU-ICFTU conflicts. One exception to this generalisation is the Sudan, where the Sudan Workers' Trade Union Federation has not merely claimed, but largely succeeded in exercising, a highly centralised form of control over its affiliated unions.(8) Finally, the fact that British African unions are concerned less with *equality* of rights, and more with the rights of *African* workers as such, necessarily gives their demands a strongly nationalist flavour, and makes it natural that they should seek to ally themselves with nationalist political parties and congresses. Even in the Sudan, where the trade-union movement has so far been successful in steering clear of party politics, the SWTUF committed itself at its 1951 Congress to working with other nationalist organisations to secure 'the liberation of the Sudan'.

In spite of these major differences in structure, the actual problems which confront the trade-union movements in British and French Africa are not essentially different. There is, first, the problem of organisation. In addition to the various difficulties arising out of the labour situation, African unions have to reckon with the fact that most European employers and managers bring with them, or develop in the rarefied colonial atmosphere, a nineteenth-century attitude to trade unionism: believe in individual or mass dismissals as the appropriate method of dealing with 'agitators' and 'malcontents': and are better placed to act on this belief on account of the pool of unemployed, or casually employed, African unskilled labour on which they can usually draw. In these circumstances it is not surprising that subscriptions are often irregular, membership records uncertain, union affairs in the hands of a junta; or that the mortality rate among the smaller and weaker unions should be high. What is more significant is that the use of trade-union cards, the holding of factory and branch meetings, the election of officers and delegates, respect for trade-union rules, the keeping of union minutes, should have acquired, among the better-organised unions, the sanctity of tribal custom. True, it is among a very small minority of the African working-class that this level of organisation has been achieved. According to the figures given in the table on page 118 there are in the region of 500,000 trade unionists in colonial Africa, not more than 10 per cent of the wage-earning population. But the figures are very rough estimates: in some cases (e.g. Nigeria) they are almost certainly inflated; and in any case the term 'trade unionist' lacks precise definition. What can be said with greater certainty is that in areas such as French West Africa and the Sudan, where trade unionism is relatively highly developed, at least one-quarter of African wage- and salary-earners are conscious, contributing trade unionists—a remarkably high proportion.(31)

There is, second, the problem of strategy. As always in the early history of trade unionism, great importance is attached in colonial Africa to strikes as an instrument of policy. 'Spontaneity is the primitive form of conscious-ness', and initially strikes occur spontaneously even where they are illegal—as in the Belgian Congo in 1941 and 1945,(32) and in Liberia, on the Firestone rubber plantation, in 1947—since they are the only argument with which workers can collectively press their economic claims and challenge managerial autocracy. In some cases general strikes have been the midwives of trade union-ism, and have acquired a special sanctity on that account. The Nigerian trade-union movement established itself as an effective force as a result of the six weeks' general strike in 1945. The 1947 general strike in the Sudan, the Workers' Affairs Association's first major operation, was largely successful in winning recognition for Sudanese trade unions.(8) Sometimes general strikes have been undertaken with a Utopian, Owenite end in view—"to disorganise the whole fabric of the old world, and transfer, by a sudden spring, the whole political government of the country from the master to the servant". The Gold Coast general strike of January 1950 was essentially a strike of this sort, called by the Gold Coast TUC in support of the Convention People's Party's campaign of 'Positive Action' and demand for 'Self-government Now'; a strike which was politically useful to the CPP, but left the trade-union movement seriously weakened.

With the development of a more mature trade-union movement, the use of the general strike of indefinite duration for revolutionary political objectives falls somewhat into the background. More emphasis comes to be placed upon local strikes, in support of limited objectives, primarily, of course, wage increases—but also for improvements in working conditions, social security measures (e.g. family allowances in French Africa), or the replacement of dismissed workers. Increasing sophistication begins to be shown in the choice of variations on the strike theme: e.g. the 'go-slow' strike, a method used by Enugu mineworkers in 1949 and by Nigerian railwaymen in 1951; guerilla twenty-four-hour, two-day and three-day general strikes, which have become a recognised trade-union technique in French West Africa and the Sudan.(33) At this stage the strike is generally still regarded as the principal weapon in the trade-union armoury, not only because of its obvious appeal to workers whose standard of life is extremely depressed, but also because of its proved effectiveness. (In French West Africa it is clear that strikes have helped to secure substantial improvements in the level of real wages since 1945.)(31) There is, moreover, a quasi-Syndicalist reason why

African trade unions, dealing with a European Government or private employer, often prefer strikes to negotiation: they may be thought of as instruments not merely to secure economic concessions for wage-earners, but also to wear down, and eventually eliminate, the colonial régime by a policy of permanent aggression.

Strikes, even when successful, can quickly exhaust the moral and organisational, as well as financial, resources of a youthful trade-union movement. Fortunately African unions have begun to develop other forms of activity and techniques of bargaining. In French Africa the *Code du Travail* makes elaborate provision for the negotiation of collective agreements between trade unions and employers' associations, covering a wide range of topics— wage scales, overtime rates, rates for women and young persons, paid holidays, the appointment of shop stewards, length of notice, etc. Even before the *Code du Travail* made such agreements obligatory, they had been brought into operation in a number of industries in French West Africa. For example, the 1952 collective agreement covering drivers in the French Sudan lays down that, during periods of absence from home, allowances for meals and overnight expenditure shall be paid at a fixed rate.(34) Case work likewise has come to be an important part of the duties of African trade-union leaders and officials—taking up cases of supposed wrongful dismissal or failure to pay full earnings with the employer concerned, or with the Labour Department or *Inspection du Travail*. Much of the loyalty which the better-organised unions are able to command depends in practice upon the efficiency with which they handle grievances of this kind. Another sign of maturity is the development of trade-union journals and bulletins—*Prolétaire* (CGT) and *Liaison* (CFTC) in Senegal, *Barakéla* (CGT) in the French Sudan—which

combine union propaganda with news items, reports
of conferences and negotiations, policy discussions,
and now and then a poem in the tradition of romantic
radicalism:

*"L'invasion barbare son oeuvre a accompli:*
*De la traite des Nègres à l'exploitation des matières*
*premières,*
*L'Afrique dépeuplée de plus de vingt millions*
*d'hommes, appauvrée et brisée*
*Comme un petit enfant sous le poids du fardeau,*
*souffre, pleure."*

There is also the problem of leadership. Trade-union
leaders in post-war Africa have been extremely varied in
origins, character, capacity and outlook. The original
leadership of the WAA in the Sudan was drawn from a
group of skilled workers in the mechanical department of
the Sudan railways. In some cases intellectuals, like Dr.
Endeley, formerly President of the Cameroons Development Corporation Workers' Union, now Leader of the
Government in the British Cameroons, have recognised
how a large union in a small country could serve the ends
of political power. There have also been workers, like
Mr. Pobee Biney, an engine-driver from Sekondi in the
Gold Coast, or Mr. Siaka Stevens in Sierra Leone, who,
during the period of transition to self-government, have
become parliamentarians or ministers. While some former leaders have become detached from trade unionism
through promotion, or courses of study in Europe, others
can say, like M. K. Basile Gnasounou Ponoukoun, of the
Dahomey CFTC: "I don't regret that the fact of these
struggles has prevented me from getting promotion since
the union was formed."(35) Some, like M. Abdoullaye

Diallo of the French Sudan, and M. Jacques N'Gom of the French Cameroons, are workers who have absorbed Marxism, and have come to play a leading part in the French CGT and the WFTU. Others, like Mr. B. O. Ojiyi, former Secretary of the Enugu Colliery Workers' Union (severely censured by the Fitzgerald Commission for his part in the strike that led up to the Enugu shootings in November 1949), himself a hewer, conform more to the traditional chiefly pattern: a 'wizard', who built up a great reputation for himself by the wage increases which he won for his miners, and came in time to dominate the mine management as well as his own union; drawing no very clear distinction between trade-union funds and his private purse—a patriarchal attitude which later led to his imprisonment. "The worthless Ojiyi" is the description given him in the Fitzgerald Report.(36) Yet, from the standpoint of the Enugu miners, he was clearly worth a good deal. Naturally trade unions in a society which offers new opportunities for the rapid acquisition of wealth and power are liable to be used at times by men whose main interest is money-making or a political career. What is interesting is that, at least in British and French West Africa, in Northern Rhodesia and the Sudan, trade unions should have begun to throw up their own leaders —distinct in background, experience and ideas from the professional and business élites.

The development of African trade unions, even on the present restricted scale, can influence the character and outlook of African nationalism in important ways. They are a means of providing political education, in the broadest sense, for a section of the community that has little opportunity to play a prominent part in nationalist political parties. They tend to substitute a new relationship based upon common economic interests for traditional tribal ties. At the same time they make it possible for the collectivist values of traditional African society to be restated in modern language, in opposition to the naïve Benthamism (or Burnhamism) of many Westernising nationalists. Or—to put the same point differently—they counteract the nationalist tendency to present political independence, or liberation from European control, as an end in itself; and draw continual attention to the facts of poverty, hunger, disease, slums, insecurity and social waste, which will not be altered simply by the transfer of political power from Europeans to Africans.

# 5

## PARTIES AND CONGRESSES

POLITICAL associations of various types have evolved in modern Africa. They include self-appointed committees of intellectuals, advocating limited reforms; pressure-groups, constructed by particular interests— chiefly, religious, regional, economic—for purposes of political action; *mafias* and underground movements, seeking to displace the colonial State, and using, or prepared to use, violence and armed revolt for the purpose; loosely organised 'congresses', demanding national independence or democratic rights; and, finally, political parties in a stricter sense—i.e. associations possessing a definite machine, a constitution and a platform, working within the framework of some kind of parliamentary system, and concerned to win the support of an electorate. It is parties in this sense that I wish mainly to consider in this chapter—their origins, structure and functions— since the rise of political parties has been one of the most interesting developments in the period since the Second World War, affecting the seventy million Africans living in the belt of tropical Africa which stretches from Dakar to Port Sudan and from Tibesti to Brazzaville. But even the most tentative discussion of African political parties must involve some account of the more primitive forms of association from which they have sprung.

Such political associations as existed in pre-war colonial Africa, though sometimes described as 'parties', were examples for the most part of what M. Duverger has

called an 'archaic and prehistoric' type of party, consisting of 'followers grouped around an influential protec-
tor'.(1) This description seems to fit such organisations as
the Aborigines' Rights Protection Society in the Gold
Coast, founded in 1897, and dominated during the inter-
war period by that remarkable Cape Coast lawyer, Mr.
W. E. G. Sekyi; (2)(3) the Nigerian National Democratic
Party, founded in Lagos in 1923, and led by Mr. Herbert
Macaulay, a civil engineer;(4) the Senegalese *section* of
the French Socialist Party (SFIO), organised and led
during the 1930s by M. Lamine Gueye, a Wolof lawyer
and *docteur en droit*;(5) or the White Standard League in
the Anglo-Egyptian Sudan, established in 1923 by Ali
Abdel-Latif, an Arabised Dinka.(6) The National Congress of British West Africa (1920), in which the moving
spirit was Mr. J. E. Casely Hayford, a distinguished Gold
Coast lawyer and journalist, belongs essentially to the
same category, though wider in scope, in that it included
representatives from all the four British West African
territories.(7)

These early political associations had certain common
characteristics. They were controlled by a small professional élite—in many cases by lawyers. (There are several
good reasons for the predominance of lawyers in the early
stages of nationalist politics. They, more than others,
have learned to express themselves in the magical language of the foreign rulers. They are trained to handle
the kind of practical problems, of a semi-legal character,
with which first-generation nationalists find themselves
faced—land, civil liberties, chiefly prerogatives, and the
like. And they, almost alone among intellectuals, can enjoy economic independence and a good deal of leisure in
a society in which most careers open to talents lie within
the Government service.) The influence of these associa-

tions was effectively limited to a few main towns—Dakar, Bathurst, Freetown, Accra, Lagos, Calabar, Khartoum-Omdurman. In West Africa they "tended more and more to be exclusive clubs for the professional and prosperous business classes which were now emerging".(8) In the Sudan, where no institutional channels existed through which nationalist politicians could play even a modest part in the making of Government policy; where the main nationalist demand, the freedom and unity of the Nile Valley, involved a direct challenge to British authority; and where the dominant religious tradition was Mahdist rather than Methodist—there was a tendency to turn towards radicalism, of which one outcome was the riots and repressions of 1924.(6) In British West Africa and Senegal, on the other hand, the fact that the urban professional élite had, since the end of the nineteenth century, enjoyed a recognised, if subordinate, place in the ruling institutions, encouraged a constitutional attitude on the part of the nationalist leadership. Political demands took the form of programmes of limited and realisable reforms: in British West Africa, an increase in the proportion of elected African members in local legislatures; the Africanisation of the public service and the judiciary; an accelerated tempo of educational development and the founding of West African universities. In Senegal the idea of the abolition of the *Indigénat*, and the extension of rights of citizenship, was canvassed. In fact, it could be argued that the post-1945 Governments of Britain and France largely took over and applied the Fabian ideas and programmes of the inter-war West African leadership.

A new factor in the British West African situation was the development in the middle 1930s of Youth Movements, Congresses and Leagues—stimulated in

part by the economic difficulties and employment problems of the growing African educated class, increased
by the world depression; and partly by the development of a radical nationalist Press, popular in its
appeal and 'modern' in its techniques, in which Dr.
Nnamdi Azikiwe of Nigeria and Mr. Wallace Johnson
of Sierra Leone played a leading part. These Youth Movements represented a more highly evolved form of political
association than their predecessors: from an organisational standpoint, since they appealed to a wider, though
still essentially an urban and educated, public, and were
based upon local branches in the main towns (membership of the Nigerian Youth Movement was estimated as
10,000 in 1938);(9) and from the standpoint of policies
and programmes—since they put forward explicit demands for self-government. But this was still a period
during which political associations lacked effective mass
support, and such movements of popular protest as
occurred—the Gold Coast cocoa hold-up of 1937–8, for
example—still tended to look to the traditional chiefly
élite rather than to the nationalist politicians for leadership.(10)

The story of the many varied factors which contributed
to transform the political situation in Africa during and
after the Second World War is too familiar to require
detailed repetition here: the democratic, anti-Fascist
(and therefore, by implication, anti-imperialist) propaganda of the United Nations; the weakening of European
imperial authority in Asia; the experience of African ser-
vicemen in the various theatres of war; the stimulus to
nationalism arising out of economic hardships, restrictions and rising prices.(11) One aspect of the new situation which has had a special bearing on the development
of political organisations is the improvement of the

means of transport. A modern political party must be able to deploy, with reasonable ease and speed, its leaders and organisers. It must ensure a reasonable degree of central or regional control over local branches and groups. It is highly desirable (and, in the political context of French Africa, essential) to enjoy means of rapid communication between the colonial territory and the metropolitan capital. These technical preconditions of effective party organisation, propaganda and pressure, have been largely satisfied in post-war colonial Africa. It would be hard to exaggerate the revolutionary political consequences of the creation of an efficient internal and international air network. In practice this means that M. Mamadou Konaté, deputy for the French Sudan, can attend a meeting of his party executive in Bamako in the morning; take part in a session of the *Grand Conseil* at Dakar in the late afternoon; and speak in the National Assembly in Paris next day. Dr. Nkrumah, Mr. Awolowo, and Isma'il al-Azhari can combine their party, parliamentary and ministerial duties in the same way. At a less exalted level, the improvement in road communications has made it possible for the middle-rank leadership of parties— national officials, regional and district secretaries and agents—to penetrate into obscure villages, in lorries, private cars, party vans or even on bicycles. Thus party propaganda and slogans can be widely diffused, local branches established, and local grievances ventilated. The gospel is preached; new converts are won; the faithful are confirmed—even in the remoter bush.

The political associations which dominated the scene in British and French West and Equatorial Africa and the Sudan during the early post-war years conformed roughly to a common pattern—though, naturally, differences in local conditions gave rise to important divergences of aim, strategy and organisation; as well as to differences in their cycles of birth, maturity and decay. They belonged to the type referred to here as 'congresses' or 'fronts' rather than parties.(12) The main points of contrast between congresses and parties can perhaps be summarised as follows. First, the congress claims to represent 'all the people'; to embody the national will, made articulate. Its dominant concept is 'popular sovereignty', and its spiritual ancestor Jean-Jacques Rousseau. Second, structurally, the congress normally takes the form of a loosely knit, even amorphous, amalgam of local and functional organisations, grouped around a nuclear executive or working committee. Third, the strategy of the congress is, in general, aggressive—expressed in such terms as 'the struggle against imperialism', 'la lutte contre la colonialisme'—and may involve any or all of the recognised techniques of popular pressure: national boycotts, general strikes, civil disobedience, mass demonstrations, press campaigns, as well as petitions, deputations and agitation through traditional channels. The party, on the other hand, though it may still claim to represent 'the mass', or 'the best elements', of the nation, recognises that there are other parties and groupings, as well as the colonial administration, with which it has to compete for power. It attempts to achieve a more tightly knit, pyramidical structure, with its basis in local branches and individual party members (though there are important differences, discussed later, in the point to which this articulation is carried). And its strategy is, in most cases, more flexible and gradualist—directed towards the use of electoral machinery and representative institutions as the main means of securing or retaining political power.

These contrasts between congresses and parties have been presented schematically. In practice, of course, the distinctions are much less clear-cut. But in both cases there is an evident connection between theory, organisation and strategy. It will be worth while to consider briefly some actual congresses from these three points of view.

In the Sudan the Graduates' General Congress was formed as early as 1937, but did not publicly commit itself to definite political demands until April 1942.(6) The National Council of Nigeria and the Cameroons (NCNC) arose out of a 'national convention' held on the initiative of the Nigerian Students' Union in August 1944.(13) The *Rassemblement Démocratique Africain* (RDA) in French Africa was established at the Bamako Conference in October 1946.(14) The United Gold Coast Convention (UGCC) was set up in August 1947.(3) These organisations were thus all, effectively, products of the political ferment which accompanied the later stages of the Second World War and continued into the early postwar period. They referred back, consciously, to the belief in the rights of subject nations which the War and the Resistance had reawakened. (RDA in fact used to point the comparison between French experience under the Germans and African experience under the French.) The original central demands of the Graduates' Congress, the NCNC and the UGCC followed a common pattern: the issue of a joint British-Egyptian declaration, "guaranteeing the Sudan, in its geographical boundaries, the right of self-determination directly after the war"; "internal self-government for Nigeria, whereby the people of Nigeria and the Cameroons under British Mandate shall exercise executive, legislative and judicial powers"; "self-government for the peoples of the Gold Coast at the earliest possible opportunity". The RDA, working within a different political and constitutional framework, evolved a somewhat different, less separatist, formula: "Equality of political and social rights . . . local democratic assemblies; and a freely agreed union of the peoples of Africa and the people of France." But through all these pronouncements runs a common theme: the notion of a people, or group of peoples, who collectively claim the right to manage their own affairs and to determine the future basis of their relationship with the metropolitan country.

The terms which these bodies used to describe themselves—'Congress', 'National Council', 'Convention', '*Rassemblement*'—have a certain significance. They imply a notion of universality—the idea that the organisation does really express the 'general will', and has a moral right to challenge the legal authority of the Administration on that account. Even the Sudan Graduates' Congress (the word 'congress', here and elsewhere in colonial Africa, has obvious Indian associations), which might seem from its title to be an élite organisation, opened its membership from 1943 on to ex-primary-schoolboys, and stressed its right to speak for the Sudanese nation. This conception—of an all-embracing, fully representative 'national front'—is brought out particularly clearly in the RDA's description of itself as "a broad political organisation, including within itself all sorts of ideology; open to every national group, to men of all social conditions, and every Territory, grouped around a programme of concrete, definite aims".(15)

Structure is related to function. Congresses, because they claim to represent 'all the people', try to build up connections of some kind with 'all the people'. This is essential, if only to avoid the traditional reproach of all colonial administrations—that the nationalist leadership speaks only for itself and a small group of urban, educated 'malcontents'; with the corollary that the true interpreters of the popular will are District Officers and loyal chiefs.(16) But the type of organisation which the congress leadership—the General Staff—builds up is usually less in the nature of a disciplined army than a congeries of irregular guerilla bands, each with its own captain, associated with the leadership by ties of sentiment and loyalty. This may mean that the congress is actually constituted on a federal basis. For example, the 1945 Constitution of the NCNC explicitly stated that "tribal unions, trade unions, political parties, professional associations, social and literary clubs, etc. (as distinct from single individuals), shall be eligible for membership of the National Council".(13) And at the height of its influence, in 1945, the NCNC had in fact about 180 such affiliated organisations. The congress may also develop its own local branches: the RDA, thanks partly to methods of organisation learned from the French Communist Party, maintained an efficient system of local committees, in the villages as well as the towns, in the regions of its greatest influence—e.g. the Ivory Coast and the French Sudan. But the tendency of congresses is to find their rank-and-file, and their subordinate commanders, in the various existing popular associations and movements, which can be called upon in times of crisis—as in Nigeria in 1945, in the Gold Coast in 1948, or in the Ivory Coast in 1949—and which, on their side, can call for support from the congress leadership.

Congress strategy is frequently aggressive, for the simple reason that it seeks to bring about a fundamental, and fairly rapid, change in the power relationships between Africans and Europeans; and the congress emerges at a time when the colonial Power shows little inclination to permit such a transformation to occur. Hence congress leaders, although they may—like Mr. Herbert Macaulay in Nigeria, Dr. Danquah in the Gold Coast, M. Houphouet-Boigny in French West Africa, or Isma'il al-Azhari in the Sudan—be far from revolutionary in their personal outlook, have accepted the necessity for the use of extra-parliamentary techniques, as a means of wearing down the resistance of the Administration. And, though they may attach importance also to the pressures which can be brought to bear through parliamentary channels, they are usually unwilling to draw nice distinctions between 'constitutional' and 'unconstitutional' methods.

Since about 1950 the initiative has tended to shift in British and French West Africa from congresses to parties. In the Sudan the activities of the Graduates' Congress became, from 1945 on, increasingly merged with those of the Ashigga Party. The regions in which congresses are still the dominant form of political association are, not surprisingly, the British East and Central African territories, in which (with the exception of Kenya) Africans enjoy limited rights of political organisation, but no form of popular suffrage, and where there is no immediate prospect of the transfer of political power from Europeans to Africans. From the standpoint of theory, structure and strategy, the Uganda, Northern Rhodesian and Nyasaland National Congresses reveal some of the characteristics discussed here(17)—as did the Kenya African Union before its suppression.(18)

What is the explanation of the decline of congresses and the rise of parties in West Africa and the Sudan? As in late nineteenth-century Europe there has been an obvious correlation between party development and the extension of the franchise. Mr. Coleman is certainly correct in describing constitutional reform as the 'precipitant' in the formation of African parties.(19) In British West Africa the years 1949 to 1951 were occupied with constitution-making. And, though the new constitutions which were eventually introduced—in 1950 in the Gold Coast, in 1951 in Nigeria and Sierra Leone—differed in important respects, all three made possible the formation of a Government, or Governments, which were predominantly African, ministerial and based upon a party, or coalition of parties, able to dominate the legislature. This was combined, in the Gold Coast and Nigeria, with taxpayers' suffrage (the effect of which was, broadly, to enfranchise women in the Gold Coast and exclude them from the franchise in Nigeria); and a system of indirect elections—outside a few main towns in which the principle of direct elections was already established. The birth of certain major West African parties—the Convention People's Party (CPP) in the Gold Coast, Action Group and the Northern People's Congress (NPC) in Nigeria, the Sierra Leone People's Party (SLPP)—can be correlated with different phases in this process of constitutional reform. In the Sudan the evolution of modern parties was stimulated by the introduction, first, of the transitional constitution of 1948, with an all-Sudanese legislature and a partially Sudanese executive; and, later, of the full-blown parliamentary system of 1953. In French Africa, while the framework of representative institutions created in 1946–7 made no provision for the transfer of executive power, it enabled Africans, through their parliamentarians and assemblymen, to enjoy some real influence over the way in which power was exercised. And, by the legislation of 1951–2, the franchise was extended to include heads of households and mothers of two children ('living or dead for France', as the rubric picturesquely puts it).(20)

Thus in mid-twentieth century Africa, as in late-nineteenth-century Europe and America, the creation of mass electorates has made necessary the evolution of modern parties as agencies for canalising popular opinion and winning popular votes. Indeed, the special conditions in which elections are held in modern Africa impose special tasks on African parties. For example, to make certain that their supporters are registered as electors, local party organisations must see that they have paid their tax and received their tax receipts. Difficulty of communications, and the distance of the remoter villages from their polling-stations, increase the importance of pre-electoral hut-to-hut canvassing. The fact that most electors are illiterate makes it essential to ensure that they are familiar with the party's symbol, where the method of voting for symbols is employed; that they are not unduly influenced by administrators or chiefs; that, as nearly as possible, the party has a local man of weight and influence in every village. In such circumstances there are strong inducements to build up parties with reasonably effective machines, from the village up to the central leadership.

There were other reasons for the decline of congresses and the rise of parties. A new generation of post-war politicians was emerging, who had studied the techniques of modern party organisation in Europe and the USA, and were dissatisfied with what seemed to be the old-fashioned agitational methods, and personal ascendancy, of the generation of nationalist leaders that the tide of revolt of the early post-war years had carried to the front. It was partly from this standpoint (in spite of important differences of outlook and theory) that M. Senghor challenged the leadership of M. Lamine Gueye in Senegal; Dr. Kwame Nkrumah challenged Dr. Danquah in the Gold Coast; and Mr. Awolowo challenged Dr. Azikiwe in western Nigeria. At the same time there were obvious difficulties in the way of maintaining the claims of the congresses to universalism, to speak on behalf of the whole nation, except during periods of acute nationalist crisis. During periods of relative quiescence the sheer breadth of the organisation—as regards both the geographical area which it attempted to cover and the various sections of opinion which it attempted to include —was often a source of embarrassment. There was a tendency for the leadership to become a junta, and for the 'mass basis' to have more meaning on paper than in fact. There was seldom an assured and regular source of funds, with the result that the congress was liable to become dependent upon the donations, and thus upon the political caprices, of a few wealthy backers.

It was primarily ideological divisions that split the RDA. At the outset, even before the Bamako Conference, the Senegalese Socialists broke away. In 1950 the conflict between the Right wing, led by the President, M. Houphouet-Boigny (and including most of the RDA parliamentary representatives), who favoured a policy of compromise with the French administration, and the Left, led by the Secretary-General, M. D'Arboussier, who favoured *la lutte à l'outrance* and continued co-operation with the French Communists, came to a head— leaving the Right in control of the machine, while the Left retained its influence in Senegal and the Cameroons, and among trade unionists and students.(21) The NCNC, on the other hand, foundered on the rock of tribalism, or communalism: it never succeeded in building up an effective organisation in the predominantly Moslem north; and in the Yoruba territories of the west it lost ground from about 1949 on because it could be represented as an Ibo-dominated body. The UGCC broke up mainly on divisions over issues of strategy and tactics between the older, *grand-bourgeois*, leadership grouped around Dr. Danquah, who believed (from 1949 on) in going slow, and the newer, *petit-bourgeois*, leadership associated with Kwame Nkrumah, who believed (at least until 1951) in forcing the pace of political change.(3) The split in the Sudanese Graduates' Congress occurred over a complex of related questions—part ideological (radicalism versus gradualism), part tactical (union with Egypt versus independence), part religious (*Khatmiyya*, supporters of Saiyid Ali al-Mirghani, versus *Ansar*, supporters of Saiyid Abder-rahman al-Mahdi).(6) Indeed, in none of these cases is it possible, by isolating a single factor, to give an adequate account of the decline of the congresses—even where one factor seems to predominate. Complete case-histories would certainly show how internal stresses and secessions were the consequence of a combination of influences—conflicts of political theory, strategy, economic and social interests; communal and regional attitudes; administrative pressures; and sheer personal rivalries.

The question of the origin of African political parties is interesting, and would repay fuller study. Some have evolved directly from earlier congresses, whose leadership has come to accept the limitations imposed by the existing constitutional framework, and has concentrated upon adapting the organisation to fit the requirements of an electoral system. This is the process which has occurred in the case of the RDA in the territories in which it was well established, and of the NCNC in southern Nigeria: in the latter case the decision of the NCNC's Kano Conference in 1951 to move over from an affiliated-organisation to an individual-member basis perhaps marked the turning-point. Other parties have arisen as a result of fission. Sometimes they have broken away from a congress —as the 'Umma Party in the Sudan broke from the

Graduates' General Congress in 1945, when the Congress passed into the control of Isma'il al-Azhari and the supporters of union with Egypt:/ (6) or as the Convention People's Party in the Gold Coast split from the UGCC in 1949, having already existed in embryo within the UGCC in the form of a 'Committee of Youth Organisations' (an example of a minority movement which succeeded in transforming itself into a majority movement).(3) Sometimes new parties have split from already established parties—the *Bloc Démocratique Sénégalais*, for example, which broke away from the Senegalese section of the French Socialist Party, on the initiative of M. Senghor and others of the younger generation of Senegalese Socialists. Some of the new communal, or regional, parties in the Gold Coast—the Moslem Association Party, the Togoland Congress, and the Ashanti National Liberation Movement—are in effect centrifugal breakaways from the CPP; and their leaders, for the most part, are drawn from the former cadres of the CPP—just as the national and local leaders of the original CPP were mainly activists who seceded with Kwame Nkrumah from the UGCC. Indeed, fissiparous tendencies, which may, given favourable circumstances, breed new political parties, are as recurrent in African as in western European parties. But in Africa the greater novelty and fluidity of the party system, and the relative weakness of party discipline, make the birth and decay of new parties and pseudo-parties more common events.

New parties can also be created through the amalgamation of splinter groups. The Ghana Congress Party in the Gold Coast was established in 1952 as a merger between the rump of the UGCC, the moderate National Democratic Party, and a few individual CPP dissidents. And in Chad the *Front pour l'Action Civique du Tchad* was formed as an electoral alliance between the local section of RDA and the local Socialists against the dominant *Union Démocratique Tchadienne*, a party enjoying the support of the tribal chiefs and the goodwill of the French Administration. This counter-tendency, towards fusion, is particularly liable to occur in the case of relatively weak opposition groups faced with a party which seems, for the time being, strongly entrenched. But it may also be a means of consolidating strength: for example, the Sudanese National Unionist Party, established in 1953 as the result of a merger between the Ashigga and other minor parties and groups supporting the principle of a constitutional 'link' with Egypt.

Many of the most effective parties, both in British and French West Africa, have been brought into being through the initiative of a semi-political association which was already well established, and could thus provide the new party with a ready-made leadership and body of support. This kind of historical connection existed between M. Houphouet-Boigny's *Syndicat Agricole Africain* and the party organised in 1945 under his direction, the *Parti Démocratique de la Côte d'Ivoire*.(22) The Kamerun National Congress (formerly the Cameroons National Federation), of which Dr. Endeley is President, had a similar link with the 11,000-strong Cameroons Development Corporation Workers' Union, reorganised on Dr. Endeley's initiative in 1947. In Nigeria Mr. Obafemi Awolowo's Action Group (1951) was the offspring of the Yoruba cultural association, *Egbe Omo Oduduwa* (i.e. 'society of the descendants of Oduduwa', the legendary ancestor of the Yorubas), a body which Mr. Awolowo inspired, created (in 1948) and led;(23) while the Northern People's Congress (1951), led by the Sardauna of Sokoto, was simply a Moslem, predominantly Hausa, cultural society—the *Jami 'a*—renamed and adapted. The Sierra Leone People's Party (1951), led by Dr. Margai, was a development from the earlier Sierra Leone Organisation Society, a body formed to promote co-operatives in the Protectorate. In all these cases continuity between the semi-political association and the fully fledged party was ensured, and a popular following carried over from the one to the other, partly through an individual leader, and the prestige, or *mystique*, which he had acquired.

Sometimes parties come into being as the result of an external stimulus. In French Africa, in particular, this is a common occurrence. The Senegalese Federation of the SFIO arose partly out of the initiative of the French Socialist Party. Outside Senegal, French Socialists have preferred to foster the growth of formally autonomous parties—partly on the ground that the SFIO is liable to appear as an alien, non-African organisation.(24) Hence, therefore, there are parties like the *Parti Progressiste Soudanais* in the French Sudan, and the *Comité d'Entente Guinéenne* in French Guinea, with what is called a 'tendance Socialiste', whose parliamentary representatives are normally *inscrits* in the Socialist group. Other major metropolitan parties have acted likewise. MRP assisted the development of the *Parti Républicain Dahoméen*. Local European supporters of the RPF (the former Gaullist party) helped to organise the *Union Démocratique Tchadienne*, as a counterblast to the radical *Parti Progressiste Tchadienne*. The French Communist Party, until 1950, gave its sympathy and support to the RDA. The part played by colonial Administrations in fostering African parties is a fascinating but obscure subject. It is at least widely believed that, particularly in the more politically backward regions of British and French

West Africa, parties representing the standpoint of the conservative nobility—e.g. NPC in Northern Nigeria, or the *Union Progressiste Mauritanienne* in Mauretania— have received official encouragement. Such parties are indeed often referred to in French Africa as 'partis de l'Administration'.(25)

Whatever the circumstances in which they have arisen, African parties are in the main extra-parliamentary in origin—having been constructed by particular individuals and groups to take advantage of a new electoral and political situation. This is not to say that intra-parliamentary influences have been without importance. The Gold Coast NPP was established on the eve of the 1954 election largely on the initiative of Northerners who had been members of the 1951–4 House of Assembly, and had realised how much the lack of parliamentary party discipline had handicapped them in their dealings with the well-organised CPP. The NPC has some of the characteristics of a club for parliamentarians from the Moslem areas of Northern Nigeria. And many parties—the Sierra Leone SLPP, for example, in 1951, and the Sudanese NUP in 1954—have acquired in Parliament new adherents whose election depended on local influence or popularity, not on party affiliation: "a phenomenon", as Mr. Coleman has pointed out, "characteristic of early party development in modern Europe".(19)

Is it possible to point to any common characteristics of these new African parties? It is necessary first to draw a broad distinction between parties with a relatively primitive, and those with a more modern, type of structure. This contrast can also be presented schematically, somewhat as follows. Parties of the former type are dominated by 'personalities', who enjoy a superior social status, either as traditional rulers or members of ruling families,

or as belonging to the higher ranks of the urban, professional élite (lawyers, doctors, etc.), or on both grounds.
Their political machinery, central and local, is of a rudimentary kind, consisting of those individuals, *chefs du
canton*, notables, men of property, who naturally gravitate
towards the party, and function, intermittently and principally at election times, as a party committee. Their
annual, or occasional, congresses are largely concerned
with giving an ovation to the party leaders and confirm-
ing them in office. They have little, if anything, in the
way of a secretariat or full-time officials : the work of running the party is regarded as a leisure-time occupation of
the party leaders. For party funds they look in the main to
wealthy backers, as need arises. They depend for popular
support less upon organisation and propaganda than on
habits of respect for traditional authority, or wealth and
reputation, among the mass (above all in the rural areas).
Thus it was said that in the 1951 election in French
Africa many of the newly enfranchised electors 'voted for
the *chef*'—voted, in other words, for the party and candidate to which the Government-appointed chief had given
his blessing. Examples of such 'parties of personalities'
are the Ghana Congress Party and Northern People's
Party in the Gold Coast; the Northern People's Congress
in Nigeria; the *Union des Chefs et des Populations du
Nord Togo* in French Togoland; the *Union Voltaïque* in
Haute-Volta; the *Union Démocratique Tchadienne* in
Chad. Such parties naturally tend to be more successful
in regions in which traditional chiefly authority has maintained itself as an effective political force—an area which
corresponds roughly, though not exactly, with the frontiers
of Islam in West and West Equatorial Africa. In the more
economically and educationally advanced coastal belt,
where habits of subordination have tended to break

down, such parties (as the failure of GCP in the Gold Coast 1954 election suggests) are faced with increasing difficulties.

Parties of the second type aim at, even if they do not always achieve, a much more elaborate structure. Since their chief claim and function is to represent the mass, they are committed to a form of organisation that is (certainly on paper, and to some extent in practice) highly democratic. The party leaders are " 'of the people' in the sense that they have achieved their positions through dint of personal talent rather than birth or privilege".(19) The basic unit of the party is the local branch (or in towns the ward); in French Africa the *comité de village* or *comité de quartier*. Above these basic units there is a pyramidical form of organisation—constituency parties, regional executives, national executive, *sous-sections* and *sections*—with the provision for election of executive committees by delegate conferences at each level. The party annual conference is a serious affair, which may last several days; it receives reports on organisation and membership, finance, Press and propaganda, youth and women's work, economic and social affairs, local government, etc.; passes numerous resolutions; defines party policy, and (if an election is approaching) approves the party's electoral programme; as well as electing the national executive committee. The local leadership of a party of this type consists, as a rule, of members of the local intelligentsia—school-teachers, clerks in Government departments or commercial firms, traders, women as well as men—most of whom are active also in other organisations, tribal unions, trade unions, farmers' associations, etc., and on this account a source of strength to the party. Parties of this type are able to achieve a much higher level of efficiency than the 'parties of personalities'; not only because they can depend upon an organised, politically conscious body of supporters, but also because they possess a continuously functioning central office (and, often also, regional and branch offices), and employ a staff of full-time party officials with administrative and organising responsibilities. Indeed, dependence upon professional politicians—*permanents*—"who naturally tend to form a class and assume a certain authority" for the running of the machine is one of the most distinctive features of the 'mass' party.(1) The cost of maintaining such a party with its central secretariat and local agents, its expenditure on offices, equipment and paperwork, is inevitably heavy; hence the need for a system of admission fees and subscriptions (which also serve to remind the individual party member that he is a party member), for frequent mass meetings with collections, and other money-raising activities. Likewise the 'mass' party must continually keep itself, its central ideas, its symbols, before the public, in the bush as well as in the towns. It therefore requires a party newspaper, or newspapers; party colours, emblems and badges; a party flag; party slogans; party rallies and *tam-tams*; party songs, ballads or hymns; and, above all in Africa, party vans. It depends for its strength not on the backing of traditional authority but upon propaganda, designed to appeal particularly to the imagination of the young, to women, to the semi-urbanised and discontented; to those who are outside the local hierarchies, and interested in reform and change.

Examples of the 'mass' party are the CPP in the Gold Coast; the NCNC in southern Nigeria; the *Bloc Démocratique Sénégalais* in Senegal; the *sections* of the RDA in the territories in which it has retained its popular influence (particularly the *Union Soudanaise* in the French Sudan,(26) and the *Parti Démocratique de la*

*Côte d'Ivoire* in the Ivory Coast); the (now illegal) *Union des Populations du Cameroun* (UPC) in the French Cameroons; the *Mouvement d'Évolution Sociale en Afrique Noire* (MESAN) in Ubangui-Shari. The Northern Elements Progressive Union (NEPU) in northern Nigeria, though restricted in its influence, is a 'mass' party in intention and structure. The Action Group in western Nigeria is something of a hybrid. It possesses some of the characteristics of a 'mass' party (formal democratic structure, emphasis on propaganda, etc.), yet has tended in practice to function as a 'party of personalities'. In any case, no actual party conforms exactly to either of these models: 'mass' parties may, when it suits them, look to traditional secular and religious leaders for support; 'parties of personalities' may equally well attempt to develop a basic branch organisation.

A third type—the 'special-interest party'—should also be mentioned. Such parties are often the expression of what Mr. Coleman has called "the process of disintegration and fragmentation . . . as a consequence of the progressive awakening of ethnic or religious minority groups", taking place in contemporary Africa.(19) One illustration is the emergence of Moslem parties in predominantly non-Moslem areas—e.g. the Moslem Association Party (MAP) in the Gold Coast. Here the ties of Islam, the demand for state-subsidised Moslem schools, and the economic grievances of Moslem immigrants from the Northern Territories and French West Africa—in general the poorest and worst-housed section of the new proletariat—have been contributory factors. The Middle Belt People's Party in Nigeria and the Ashanti National Liberation Movement in the Gold Coast might also be included among 'special-interest parties'. In the latter case the demand for a higher cocoa price, resistance to

CPP centralism, and memories of past Ashanti greatness, have combined to produce an interesting variant—a chief-sponsored 'mass' party, standing for a militant tribal nationalism. Such parties cannot as a rule hope to do more than win concessions for the limited interests they represent—and incidentally satisfy desires for political leadership among those excluded from the ruling nationalist group. But the fact that they occur is evidence of the continuing strength of particularism in contemporary Africa.

The future, one might reasonably guess, lies with the mass' parties. They therefore deserve rather closer consideration. One common characteristic is the radical character of their professed aims, set out in elaborate written constitutions, in which western democratic and socialist ideas are blended with African nationalist doctrine. CPP, for instance, states that it seeks "to serve as a vigorous conscious political vanguard for removing all forms of oppression and for the establishment of a democratic socialist society" . . . "to work with other nationalist, democratic and socialist movements in Africa and other continents, with a view to abolishing imperialism, colonialism, racialism, tribalism" . . . "to support the demand for a West African Federation and . . . Pan-Africanism by promoting unity of action among peoples of Africa and African descent."(3) BDS likewise includes among its principles "the unity of action of all Senegalese workers, irrespective of race and religion . . . with the object of eliminating classes and castes by the conquest of power and the socialisation of the means of production and exchange"; its purpose is described as "to struggle effectively against capitalist imperialism", while its method is "based on the Negro African tradition renewed by the impact of European techniques".(27) It must not be supposed that this language is evidence of Communist influence. Both Dr. Nkrumah and M. Senghor are well acquainted with Marxism, but they and the parties which they lead are committed, for the present, to policies of gradualism. The fact is rather that any African 'mass' party, if it wishes to gain popular support, must speak the language of modern radicalism.

Where does power lie in an African 'mass' party? The role of the 'leader' (the word is used also in French Africa) is clearly of extreme importance. He must at the same time be the supreme manager of the party organisation, which normally he has played a major part in creating, chief theoretician, and mainly responsible for the formulation of party strategy. He must also lead his party in the Legislative or Territorial Assembly, and serve, in British West Africa or the Sudan, as Prime Minister if his party is in power. (In French Africa the special status of the party leader, as the recognised spokesman of African popular opinion, and often a *parlementaire*, puts him in a strong position to influence the executive—either directly, or through French parliamentary channels. In Trust Territories the party leader has also the special function of representing African opinion in his dealings with the United Nations.) Most important of all, the leader has to symbolise the nationalist idea for the mass of party members and sympathisers. It is above all his duty to make his party's policy intelligible to the rank and file, a large proportion of whom are illiterate farmers, fishermen, labourers and marketwomen. He therefore necessarily acquires certain numinous qualities. He may be thought of as possessing supernatural powers. Christians will tend to regard him in Messianic terms. His role becomes partly that of the Prophet in the more primitive forms of nationalist movement—he is the new Moses who will lead his people across the Red Sea to self-government. He may even be made the object of hymns, prayers and creeds—'I believe in Kwame Nkrumah. . . .' At the same time he may inherit some of the functions of the traditional chief (in fact in some cases he may become a chief)—presiding over ceremonials, pouring libations, accessible to those with disputes to settle or injustices to be remedied, the symbol of reconciliation and unity.

In one sense the special status of the party leader is simply the consequence of the process which M. Duverger calls 'the personalisation of power'. (1) It is indeed by no means certain that Kwame Nkrumah in the Gold Coast, Nnamdi Azikiwe in southern Nigeria, Félix Houphouet-Boigny in the Ivory Coast, Léopold Sédar-Senghor in Senegal, Sylvanus Olympio in French Togoland, Ruben Um Nyobé in the French Cameroons, Barthélémy Boganda in Ubangui-Shari, enjoy, within their own parties, power that is essentially different in kind from that enjoyed by Hugh Gaitskill, Anthony Eden, or Guy Mollet. There are, though, certain differences in the situation. There is, first, the fact, already referred to, that in Africa popular attitudes towards party leaders are more obviously coloured by religious feelings (whether Christian, Moslem or Animist, or some combination of these). Second, certain types of traditional ritual—for example the reciting of heroic lays in honour of the great man by a *griot*, or professional bard, in Senegal—have been taken over and adopted as party ritual. Third, the leaders of contemporary African parties are still, in almost every case, also the founders of their parties: they therefore enjoy the special kind of prestige that attached to a Keir Hardie, a Lenin or a Jefferson. Fourth, influenced perhaps partly by American models, the tendency has been for African parties to adopt a presidential form of government. The party leader is generally also the party's President: sometimes, as in the case of Dr. Nkrumah he holds the office of Life Chairman. The Secretary-General (or the party's chief permanent official, however described) seldom appears to be able to achieve authority approaching that of the President. This is partly due, of course, to the fact that most African 'mass' parties have not yet reached a stage at which they are so firmly established that they can develop a powerful bureaucracy. One exception to this generalisation—that African parties are based upon the concept of presidential power—was the RDA, during the period when it was *apparenté* to the French Communist Party: in that situation M. Gabriel D'Arboussier, as Secretary-General, undoubtedly enjoyed a position of great influence, due not only to his management of the party's machine but also to his exceptional intellectual powers and political training. But in the conflict of 1949–50 the Secretary-General was defeated by the President. The *Union des Populations du Cameroun*, on the other hand, which retains the Left-wing orientation of the old RDA, is also still led by its Secretary-General, M. Um Nyobé.

The power-structure within the African 'mass' party does not appear to differ greatly from that of its European prototypes. Associated with the leader is some form of inner party caucus, on whose loyalty and unity of purpose the party depends for much of its effectiveness. The Nkrumah-Gbedemah-Botsio triumvirate has functioned successfully as a caucus of this kind within the CPP during the period 1951–5. At a lower level the party *militants* provide a recognisable, and relatively dependable, local leadership. These are the men and women (the participation of women is more marked in the local organisations than at the centre) who serve as chairmen, secretaries and treasurers of the party branches and *sous-sections*; who organise meetings and rallies on the occasions of visits from national party leaders; who run socials and *tam-tams*, and raise local funds; who influence the choice of the local candidate, and may even select him; who manage electoral contests; who may, particularly in British West Africa, sit on local councils; who are in touch with public opinion in their areas, understand the local grievances and alignments, and can use them for party purposes. These *militants* are indispensable people. They are for the most part men and women who have had at least a primary education; who can handle correspondence, draft documents and keep minutes in English or French; teachers, minor officials, clerks, traders and contractors—often with a tradition of 'militancy' and opposition to the European administration behind them. It is they who, in their localities, constitute the party machine.

On the periphery is a much larger body of party members and sympathisers. As in Europe, the notion of a *sympathisant*, though of great practical importance, is not easily definable:(1) a man or woman, perhaps, who sometimes reads, or has read to him, the party newspaper; who knows the party slogans and catchwords ('Freedom' in the case of the CPP, 'Islam' in the case of the MAP); who makes a practice of attending party rallies; who may sometimes contribute to party funds; and who, above all, has no doubts about his party allegiance. (His connection with his party may, of course, take the form of participation in one of the many organisations loosely associated with it—a Tribal Union, a youth association, or a religious movement—rather than in a local organ of the party itself.)(28) The most important difference between the African and the European situation in this matter is the lack of a clear distinction between the status of party members and sympathisers—due partly to the difficulty of organising a system of regular contributions, so that anyone who has once paid an initial contribution to the party, and received a party card, tends to regard himself as a party member for life. This fact partly accounts for the surprising discrepancies between European and African estimates of a party's strength. RDA in French Africa, at the height of its influence, claimed to have 'millions of sympathisers'. It still claims the support of 80 per cent of the population of the Ivory Coast. A recent estimate put its membership in French Guinea at 300,000—including children, since families frequently enrol *en bloc*—or about 13 per cent of the total population. These and similar figures are not absurd, if they are taken as referring to a mental attitude, a sense of party loyalty, rather than to an organised, formal, contributory connection.(29)

This is not the place to discuss the pathology of African parties. Indeed the evidence is not yet available on which such a discussion could be based. What is clear is that, once established and having achieved a certain measure of power, African 'mass' parties are confronted with inner organisational problems which resemble, in many respects, the problems of European parties of the Left. There is evidence of the same tendency to oligarchy, particularly of the passing of control over the party machines into the hands of parliamentarians or Assemblymen (and, in British West Africa, Ministers). The latter, as elsewhere, enjoy the important advantages which accompany management, responsibility and the control of patronage; and, even more than in Europe, the scarcity of able politicians means that promising internal leaders are quickly transformed into parliamentarians. At the same time, because these parties are themselves the products of semi-revolutionary anti-colonial movements, and because in many areas the parties are inheritors of the traditions of tribal democracy, problems of party discipline tend to be more acute in contemporary Africa than in Europe. Most 'mass' parties are faced with recurrent 'caves' and revolts, organised sometimes around the criticism of party policy by its intellectuals—a factor which led to the split in the NCNC in eastern Nigeria, and the founding of the Nigerian Independence Party (NIP), in 1953; sometimes around tribal and regional antagonisms, such as have led to defections from the CPP in Ashanti and Togoland; sometimes around a Left wing, which argues that the revolution has been betrayed, that the leadership has come to terms with 'imperialism', that luxury and corruption flourish in high places, while there is no radical improvement in the conditions of peasants and workers; sometimes from a sheer loss of dynamic, and consequent isolation of the leadership from the rank and file within the party, once the principle of self-government has been conceded, and the party's main battle-cry has thus a less immediate emotional appeal.

Though the possibility of 'one-party dominance', after the realisation of self-government, cannot be ruled out, and the totalitarian aspirations of such well-organised 'mass' parties as CPP are often referred to with alarm, there are strong influences making in a contrary direction. One is this factor of intense opposition and conflict within the party itself. Another is the existence, in most territories, of a rudimentary party system. In French Africa three fairly clear alignments have so far emerged: the Socialists and their allies; the RDA and its *sections*; and the various territorial parties (of which BDS is the most important) loosely associated in the parliamentary group, the *Indépendants d'Outre-Mer*.(30) Though there are few profound divisions on policy questions between these three groupings, each has begun to acquire the kind of mixed geographical, religious and socio-economic basis that may help to ensure survival. In a somewhat similar way the three major Nigerian parties—NPC, the Action Group and NCNC—though predominantly regional, have also become associated with reasonably well-defined interests: NPC with the Northern aristocracy and country gentry; Action Group with the prosperous, conservative, professional and trading classes of the West; and NCNC (like the Liberal Party in nineteenth-century Britain) with a combination of Eastern entrepreneurs and popular, predominantly urban, radicalism. And outside these are the minority parties, like NIP, with sound principles but lacking a solid social foundation. Moreover, there are already signs of a shift of interest, away from purely nationalist to class politics—most evident in French West Africa and the Sudan, where the Anti-imperialist Front is perhaps the first African party that is explicitly proletarian in outlook and programme. Thus parties, it can be argued, have become essentially African institutions; whatever their deficiencies, a more constructive method of canalising African political energies than Mau-Mau.

# 6

## THEORIES AND MYTHS

A<small>LL</small> political movements find a need to justify themselves; to construct 'ideologies'. This is particularly
evident in the case of relatively young movements,
such as the national movements of colonial Africa, which
cannot—like the British Conservative and Labour
Parties, for example—rely upon habits of unthinking
loyalty among a large body of hereditary supporters to
ensure their effectiveness. They have to build up new
loyalties; and, to achieve this, they have to break down
the feelings of impotence, dependence and irresponsi-
bility among Africans which it is in the nature of colonial
rule to produce. They must also weaken, or divert to their
own purposes, traditional tribal loyalties which obscure
the vision of the 'nation' which is to be. Much nationalist
propaganda (in the Press especially), which Europeans
often deplore as 'crude', 'virulent' or 'distorted', is concerned with this simple function—of restoring the confidence of Africans in their capacity for political action;
in their power, if they so choose, to affect the course
of history. Understandably, therefore, it is liable to be
emotionally highly charged, relying on rhetoric rather
than argument—like this chorus from one of the so-called
'KAU' hymns: (1) "You Europeans are nothing but rob-
bers, though you pretended you came to lead us. Go away,
go away, you Europeans, the years that are past have been
more than enough for us."

As in all colonial and semi-colonial societies since the

American War of Independence, the theoretical weapons with which African nationalists make their revolutions have been largely borrowed from the armouries of the metropolitan countries. Much of the political thinking of contemporary African leaders is bound to be derivative. They are themselves the products of European schools and universities. They are asserting claims of a kind that have already been asserted by Europeans, around which a European sacred literature has been built up. And they have to state their case in a language that will be intelligible to their European rulers. It would be possible to trace the influence of a variety of strains of Western thought. But three stand out as having had the most profound effect upon the African nationalist outlook: the Christian idea of human brotherhood and the specifically Protestant conception of an 'Elect'; the traditional democratic belief in "the right to choose our own governors, to cashier them for misconduct and to frame a government for ourselves"(2); and the Socialist (not necessarily Marxian) conception of a society in which 'economic exploitation', poverty and unemployment are abolished, and rewards are related to work. Naturally these principles are adapted to fit the African context. The chief implication of the idea of human brotherhood is the abolition of all forms of colour bar; and it is the Africans, or a given African people, who constitute the 'Elect'. It is the European governors who must be cashiered, and the Africans who must frame a government for themselves. It is above all the 'exploitation' of African workers by European capitalists and managers that must be abolished. So expressed, these ideas are intelligible, relevant and explosive.

It would, however, be a mistake to overstress the derivative element in African nationalist beliefs. Professor

Margaret Read has explained the tendency of Africans, exposed to the European impact, to move from a phase of thorough-going imitation of European culture to a phase of rediscovery and reassertion of traditional values, and the search for some form of synthesis.(3) Occasionally this interest in synthesis preceded the development of nationalism in any organised form. One remarkable example of such an interest was Sultan Njoya of the Bamum, in the Cameroons, who, early in this century, during the period of German administration, sought to provide his people with new intellectual equipment by inventing, and later refining, an ideographic Bamum script; in which he proceeded to compose a history of the Bamum people over the past seventeen reigns, and a treatise on religion, designed to reconcile the basic doctrines of Islam, Christianity and Bamum Animism.(4)

With the rise of nationalism began a more self-conscious effort to reconcile the theories underlying traditional African institutions and the new imported democratic ideas: an effort whose main practical purpose was to refute the official European view—that notions of political rights and representative government were foreign to Africa, unsuitable for transplantation to tropical climates. The nationalists' answer was to insist that the new parliamentary democratic institutions, for which they were beginning to press, amounted in fact to nothing more than an adaptation to new conditions of the traditional, and essentially democratic, forms of political system which were to be found in most parts of pre-European Africa. This is a point to which the late Mr. Casely Hayford, the intellectual leader of Gold Coast nationalism during the first quarter of the present century, used continually to return in his speeches and writings:

"A people who could, indigenously, and without a litera-ture, evolve the orderly representative government which ob-tained in Ashanti and the Gold Coast before the advent of the foreign interloper, are a people to be respected and shown consideration when they proceed to discuss questions of self-government."(5)

Forty years later this heresy had become orthodoxy in the Gold Coast. In 1949 the Coussey Committee, recommend-ing the introduction of a system of parliamentary govern-ment, could quote as sound doctrine Mr. Martin Wight's view that "there is no intrinsic disharmony between the indigenous institutions of the Gold Coast and the im-ported Western representative system. . . . Both embody the representative principle and both are government by discussion."(6)

The appeal to African history is indeed a theme which runs through contemporary nationalist thinking and argument. Since Byron reminded the Greeks of Sappho and Marathon every nationalist myth has included this element of reference back to past greatness. "You cannot have a nation without ancestors." But, while it was natural for Arab nationalists to look back to the early Caliphate, and Indians to Akbar, for Africans the redis-covery and reconstruction of their history has special im-portance. No western European seriously questioned the fact that there had been periods in the past when Arab and Indian civilisations, owing little to European stimu-lus, flowered—though they might question the argument that those who claimed to be the successors to these civilisations were capable of governing themselves in the conditions of the modern world; that past achievement was evidence of present capacity. But the case of the peoples of Africa south of the Sahara is different. They, according to the conventionally accepted European myth,

are 'people without a history', who, until the period of
European colonisation were 'living in the Stone Age'.
The primitive level of their techniques can be demonstrated by the fact that 'they never invented the wheel'
and 'never developed the art of writing'. Intellectually
they are 'children', members of 'the only race which has
contributed nothing to humanity'.(7) A picturesque expression of this stereotype is to be found in a pamphlet,
*African Opportunity*, by Lord Milverton, a former
Governor of Nigeria:

". . . The African has had self-government. Until about
fifty years ago he had had it for countless centuries, and all it
brought him was blood-stained chaos, a brief, insecure life,
haunted by fear, in which evil tradition and custom held him
enslaved to superstition, hunger, disease, squalor and ruth-
less cruelty, even to his family and friends. For countless centuries, while all the pageant of history swept by, the African
remained unmoved—in primitive savagery."

Faced with this heavy artillery, African nationalists
have been compelled to develop their own counter-
attack; to answer the myth of African barbarism and
backwardness with the counter-myth of African civilisation and achievement. This answer has taken various
forms. One is a new emphasis upon Egypt and the Nile
Valley, the home of the most ancient African civilisation,
which—it is sometimes suggested—was also a Negro
African civilisation, and starting-point of the wanderings
that peopled much of modern Africa.(8) Another is the re-
newal of interest in the chain of States that flourished in
the mediaeval Sudan (whose recorded history has been
partly preserved in the writings both of Arabs and
Africans)—Ghana, Mali, Gao, the Mossi kingdom, the
Hausa States, Kanem, Wadai, the Fung kingdom(9)—and
particularly in their vigorous commercial and intellectual

life; in their heroic kings, like Mansa Musa, the four-teenth-century Emperor of Mali,(10) and their outstanding scholars, like Ahmad Baba, who taught in the late sixteenth century in the University of Sankoré, at Timbuktu.(11) In the same way the process of reinterpreting the past has begun to be applied to the period of European penetration and conquest. African leaders of the resistance to European power—like the Sudanese Mahdi, Muhammad Ahmad, El-Hajj Omar, the Toucouleur,(12) or King Ja-Ja of Opobo—conventionally represented as fanatics or tyrants, can be transformed into heroes of the drama of African liberation, to whose essential beliefs the present generation of nationalist leaders has succeeded. Thus the latter no longer appear as upstarts and pretenders, but as inheritors of an honourable tradition. But perhaps the most important, and deeply felt, aspect of the nationalist answer to the myth of African barbarism is the new stress placed on the qualities of pre-European African societies: their achievements in such fields as the plastic arts, work in gold and bronze and ivory, music and dancing, folk story and folk poetry; the complexity and depth of their religious beliefs and metaphysics; their conception of the community—as 'consisting of the dead, the living and the unborn'; their rational attitude to sexual relations and to the place of women in society—their delight in children and reverence for the aged; their view of education, as a process continuing through life; their dislike of autocracy, and their delicate political mechanisms for securing the expression and adjustment of different interests and wills.(13)

When history begins to be thought of in this instrumental way, inevitably a strain of romanticism appears. If the apologists for European rule present this Hobbesian picture of a pre-European Africa in which there was "no account of Time; no Arts; no Letters; no Society; and which is worst of all, continuall feare, and danger of violent death; And the life of man, solitary, poore, nasty, brutish, and short"(14)—it is natural that the advocates of African self-government should reply with a Rousseauian picture of an African golden age of perfect liberty, equality and fraternity. The Hobbesian myth, taken literally, is nonsense. But the nationalist counter-myth involves the same tendency to hypostatise 'the African past', when there are in fact many diverse African pasts. What is important, however, is that this process of rewriting African history, outside the familiar framework of colonial preconceptions, is taking place on an increasing scale. It has been due largely to the work of such men as Sir Apolo Kagwa(15) in Buganda, Samuel Johnson(16) in western Nigeria, J. M. Sarbah(17) in the Gold Coast, in the last generation, and Dr. J. B. Danquah,(18) the Abbé Alexis Kagamé in Ruanda-Urundi,(19) and the group of French African writers associated with *Présence Africaine* in this, that the young African élite has rejected the simple equations—"all that is European is civilised; all that is African is barbarous". Indeed they take for granted that they also have inherited complex and interesting civilisations, which can be enjoyed and respected. But this new awareness of history, while it permeates all forms and levels of nationalist thought, itself provides no positive basis for a theory—or rather, it can be used to support many types of theory: equalitarian (Dr. Azikiwe) or aristocratic (M. Fily Dabo Sissoko); traditionalist (Dr. Danquah) or revolutionary (M. D'Arboussier); tribalist (Mr. Awolowo) or Pan-African (Dr. Nkrumah); Africanophil (Mr. Kenyatta) or Westernising (M. Senghor).

The contemporary African renaissance, which has naturally developed furthest in those territories where political nationalism is most firmly established, has an effect upon practice as well as upon attitudes. Superficially it shows itself in the fact that, increasingly, educated Africans abandon shorts and shirts and return to traditional clothes—for parties and ceremonies, if not for everyday use; prefer tribal to Christian names; marry according to 'native custom'; pour libations; drink palm-wine and home-brewed beer; take pleasure in traditional forms of music and dancing. The use of 'Ghana', a term charged with patriotic emotions, as the semi-official name of the Gold Coast (however tenuous the actual historic connections of the modern Gold Coast with the ancient Ghana kingdom), is another manifestation of the same attitude.(20) More fundamental is the effort to find new artistic forms through which old popular themes can be expressed—illustrated by M. Keita Fodeba's *Théâtre Africaine* in French West Africa, or the fantasies of Mr. Amos Tutuola, the Yoruba writer. And, as in every other national renaissance, there has been a developing interest in the use of vernaculars for purposes of literary and scientific expression (in many of them—e.g. Hausa, Yoruba, Fante, Luganda—a substantial amount of writing does go on). Recently M. Cheikh Anta Diop has demonstrated the flexibility of Wolof by his translations of Racine, Marx and Einstein;(8) and Mr. E. S. Asamoa has urged the need to accept some form of basic Akan as the national language of the Gold Coast.(21) In fact most nationalists would probably agree with M. Sartre, that the movement for African liberation is, in one of its aspects, a struggle to break out of the 'prison-house' of alien languages and cultures which Europe has imposed:

"Like the scholars of the sixteenth century who understood each other only in Latin, the Blacks rediscover themselves only on the terrain full of traps which White men have set for them. . . . This syntax and this vocabulary, forged in another time, in thousands of places, to answer to other needs and to designate other objects, are inadequate to provide [the Negro] with the means to speak of himself, of his cares or of his hopes."(22)

It is worth considering what have been the influences which have contributed to this African renaissance. One certainly has been the work of the social anthropologists over the past fifty years, who have exposed the curious muddle of meanings associated with such terms as 'civilised' and 'primitive', 'advanced' and 'backward'; who have shown how it is possible for an intricate and carefully balanced system of political relationships and a mature ethic to coexist with a relatively simple economy and a low level of technological development. While it has not been the anthropologist's responsibility to point a moral, no African (and no intelligent European) could read Père Tempels' *La Philosophie Bantoue*, or the collection of essays, *African Worlds*—to take two recent examples—and continue to accept the myth of African barbarism.

The archaeologist's contribution has been important too. It was at one time the fashionable view that any remarkable work of art or architecture discovered in Africa south of the Sahara must have been produced by non-Africans—Arabs perhaps, probably Portuguese—since Africans were by definition incapable of this level of achievement. This was the only way in which Europeans could account for the sculptures of Ife and Benin, the castles of Gondar, the fortifications of Zimbabwe, without disturbing their preconceptions. Now the archaeological evidence has led to a rejection of this *a priori* reasoning in each case. Moreover, the work of French and

British archaeologists, both in West and East Africa, has made it possible to begin to reconstruct more adequately the remoter periods of pre-European history; has thrown light on movements of population, communications and processes of technical change within Africa, as well as upon relations between Africa and Asia, before the coming of the Portuguese.(9) If the inhabitants of the Nigerian Plateau were producing the admirable *Nok* sculptures, and Aksum was trading peacefully with India, at a time when the British were being slowly civilised by the Romans, what is left of the myth of Africans as a 'people without a history'?

Other factors have influenced this African renaissance. The profound effect of African forms in the plastic arts upon Europe has helped to loosen the hold of the myth that 'Africans have contributed nothing to humanity'. The secondary schools of British Africa—Achimota in the Gold Coast, for example—have encouraged the enjoyment of African music and dancing, African work in sculpture and painting, and the use of African dress. Indigenous African schools of painting have developed—around M. Lodz in Brazzaville and the late M. Desfossés in Elisabethville. In French West Africa the *Institut Français d'Afrique Noire*, through its research and publications, has helped to make Africans aware of the wealth, diversity and possibilities of African-centred studies. In some ways most important of all—educated Africans have been quick to detect the inconsistencies in colonial mythology. As Professor Kahin has pointed out, in his account of the genesis of the Indonesian national movement:

"Even the student who limited his reading to the curriculum could not help noting that the dominant strain in Dutch national ideology was independence from outside control, and found it hard not to see a parallel between an upholder of Dutch power in the Indies, such as Van Heutz, and the Duke of Alba. Likewise he found it difficult, in view of Dutch national history, to understand why the history books on Indonesia which he was given painted Diponegoro and other leaders of resistance to the Dutch as worthless traitors and selfish opportunists."(23)

This account could with equal justice be applied to Africa. African nationalists believe that they have probed what are called 'Western values', and detected the confusions of thought which the words are intended to conceal. Belief in brotherliness—but not in the field of interracial relations. Belief in reason—with the prevalence of occultism and superstition. Belief in the supreme importance of the individual—with preparation for wars in which humanity can be annihilated. In this situation it is natural for Africans to feel themselves thrust back upon their own intellectual and moral resources, compelled to look increasingly to Africa rather than to Europe for their foundations.

The argument so far would suggest that the solid basis of African nationalism is the revolt against European colonial theory; that it has not as yet produced any widely accepted alternative theory, or dominant theoretician. There is no African Mazzini; no Gandhi or Sun Yat-Sen. This is not surprising. African nationalism differs from the nationalisms of India and China in that Africa exists as an idea only, projected into the future, not as an historic fact. There has been no single comprehensive civilisation, no common background of written culture, to which nationalists could refer. Africa contains a multiplicity of peoples, at very different levels of social development. Only during the present century has it become possible for Africans to think of themselves as 'Africans', with a certain community of interests and claims. What is important is that Africans do increasingly think of themselves in this way; and have begun to search for some form of unifying belief, or set of beliefs, which will do justice to the common elements in African experience: the sense of community derived from traditional society; the fact of subjection to European power, first through the Slave Trade, and later through the partition of Africa; endurance of the colour bar in all its varied manifestations.

The use of Ethiopian symbolism is one example.(24) The term 'Ethiopian', traditionally used to refer to the darker-skinned peoples in general ('Away, you Ethiop!') and Africans in particular, seems first to have become associated with ideas of liberty and liberation early in the nineteenth century, at a time when the Negro anti-slavery movement was developing in America and the West Indies. (For example, Mr. Robert A. Young's *Ethiopian Manifesto, Issued in defence of the Black Man's Rights, in the Scale of Universal Freedom,* New York, 1829.) The value of 'Ethiopia' as a symbol of Negro and African emancipation was enhanced by Biblical authority, particularly the often-quoted 68th Psalm: "He hath scattered the peoples that delight in war. Princes shall come out of Egypt; Ethiopia shall haste to stretch out her hands unto God." Thus it was natural for Africans to describe the separatist Churches emerging, in South Africa and elsewhere, at the end of the nineteenth century as 'Ethiopian' Churches. The identification of 'Ethiopia' with 'liberated Africa' was made easier by increasing African knowledge about, and interest in, the kingdom of Ethiopia. After the partition of Africa by the European Powers, and more particularly after the Italian defeat at the battle of Adowa in 1896, this other Ethiopia acquired special importance in African eyes as the one surviving independent African State. The fact that this State possessed an ancient monarchy, a national Christian Church with an older tradition than many European Churches, an indigenous written language and script, as well as an ancient liturgical language and a sacred literature, helped to increase its prestige at a time when Africans were experiencing the full shock of European conquest, and were beginning to search for an answer to the myth of African inferiority. (This attitude was reflected in the various attempts, from the end of the nineteenth century on, by South African 'Ethiopian' Church leaders to enter into relations with the Church of Ethiopia.) Thus Ethiopia, the living exemplar of an unconquered, historic African people, and 'Ethiopia', the idea of a future liberated Africa, coalesced: the one symbol came to bear a dual meaning.

The idea of general African liberation has been expressed also in terms of 'Pan-Africa'—i.e. the concept of the eventual union of all African peoples in a single State. Whether anything sufficiently solid and coherent to be described as a 'Pan-African movement' yet exists is questionable. But at least since the end of the First World War—stimulated by Garveyism and the prevailing doctrine of self-determination—a Pan-African idea has existed and influenced the outlook of the more radical African nationalists. Initially the main impetus came from the Negro community in the United States—from the writings and organising work of such men as Dr. W. E. Burghardt Du Bois; but increasingly the initiative has passed into African hands. Periodic Pan-African Congresses have been held—the first in Paris in 1919, at the time of the Peace Conference, under the Presidency of the Senegalese deputy, M. Blaise Diagne;(25) Pan-African literature published; and Pan-African policies advocated by such African politicians as Dr. Azikiwe in Nigeria, Dr. Nkrumah in the Gold Coast, Mr. Kenyatta in Kenya, and Mr. Nkumbulah in Northern Rhodesia. In French Africa the theory, as essentially separatist, is rejected by most of the older generation of political leaders. But many of the younger generation seem inclined to accept the view that "nowadays the policies of the most intelligent African leaders are explicitly Pan-African".(26) M. Cheikh Anta Diop, for example, argues that "only the existence of independent African States, federated around a democratic central government—from the Libyan coast of the Mediterranean to the Cape, from the Atlantic to the Indian Ocean—will enable Africans to develop fully and make themselves respected."(8) Independence on anything less than a Pan-African scale, M. Diop suggests, would mean the creation of relatively weak African States, still in practice dependent upon external Powers.

It is not always easy to distinguish between Pan-African and Pan-Negro (or 'Pan-Melanist') ideas. Pan-Africanism is, however, a fairly precise geopolitical concept, according to which the future United States of Africa is usually conceived as including the admittedly non-Negro peoples of Egypt and North Africa. Pan-Negrism is more in the nature of a *mystique*, which directs its appeal to Negroes (and coloured people) wherever they may be—including the Negro communities of America and the West Indies. Like Pan-Slavism or Pan-Turanism, Pan-Negrism depends for its effectiveness not so much upon a political programme as on a metaphysic —the belief that the Negro peoples of the world are the carriers of certain values, and that the assertion of these values is bound up with the cause of Negro emancipation, not simply from colonial rule, but from all forms of racial discrimination and oppression. The term coined to express this sense of a common Negro inheritance and destiny, among French Africans and *Antillais*, is *Négritude*. The most interesting exposition of the metaphysic of *Négritude* is to be found in M. Sartre's brilliant dithyramb, *Orphée Noir*. For M. Sartre *Négritude* is essentially a revolutionary concept, reflecting the status of the Black people as the proletariat of the world. It includes such elements as the idea of liberty as earned through suffering:

"To the absurd utilitarian agitation of the White the Black opposes the long authenticity of his suffering. . . . The Black represents himself in his own eyes as the man who has taken upon himself all human misery and who suffers for all, even for the White."

Belief in the enjoyment of nature as more valuable than sheer technical efficiency:

"Césaire properly calls us 'conquerors, omniscient and naïve'. Of technique the White knows all. But this merely scratches the surface of things; it is unaware of the substance, of the life within. Negritude, on the contrary, is a comprehension through sympathy."

Belief in the abolition of racial privilege as the universal mission of the Negro peoples:

"The Negro creates an anti-racist racism. He does not at all wish to dominate the world . . . he affirms his solidarity with the oppressed of all colours."

M. Senghor has on various occasions emphasised a rather different aspect of *Négritude*. In his view the great achievement of the African and Negro peoples has been *la sagesse*—the art of living: expressed through their democratic social structures; their religion; their attitude to birth, marriage and death; their work; their arts; their rhythms; which together make up "les divers aspects d'une même activité vitale, qui est la sagesse".(27)

There are many politically-minded Africans, no doubt, for whom this conception of *Négritude* appears as a form of mystification, or 'bourgeois romanticism';(28) just as there are others for whom Pan-Africanism represents a sample of Utopian political thinking; and others for whom Ethiopianism is simply a crude symbolism which has grown up around the separatist Churches. None the less all three themes have real contemporary importance, since they serve, in different ways, to make Africans more conscious of a certain community of interests and experience, in respect of which they can legitimately regard themselves as Africans; as well as to suggest that the issues raised by the various limited, territorial national movements are also continental, and even universal, in character.

*PART III*

# EPILOGUE

A T this stage it seems worth while suggesting not so much conclusions as working hypotheses about the present state and future prospects of African nationalism. At least they may provide some basis for discussion.

1. The national movements which have developed in Africa, south of the Sahara and north of the Union, for all their diversity do seem to possess certain common characteristics.

2. The common object—with minor variations—of these movements is the creation of self-governing States in which political power will rest, effectively, with Africans. The presence in particular territories of resident non-African minorities does not materially affect the nationalist objective, though it may have important consequences for nationalist strategy.

3. The tempo of development of nationalist organisations and consciousness since the last war has been remarkably rapid—particularly, but not only, in British and French West Africa and the Sudan. Since most of the long-term factors which appear to have contributed to that development—urbanisation, educational advance, external stimuli, etc.—are likely to continue to operate, there is no reason to expect any slowing down in this tempo.

4. Whether national movements in particular territories employ violent or non-violent, revolutionary or constitutional, methods to gain their objects seems likely to depend primarily upon the attitudes of the colonial régimes, the flexibility of their policies, their willingness

to make substantial political concessions, and generally upon tactical considerations.

5. The fact that self-governing African States have already begun to emerge is liable to produce—and is already producing—a chain-reaction, stimulating nationalist consciousness and organisation in territories which remain under colonial rule.

6. The social and political system which exists in the Union of South Africa, and the concept of *Apartheid* with which it has come to be associated, are normally regarded by African nationalists both as the most powerful opposing force with which they are confronted, and as a symbol of the colonial idea in its most highly developed form.

7. The tendency of European minorities in East and Central Africa (including the Belgian Congo) to seek forms of closer association with one another, and with ruling groups in the Union of South Africa, has the effect of encouraging African nationalist leaders throughout colonial Africa (and the Union) to establish closer links between their respective national movements: to give, in fact, more effective organisational form to Pan-African ideas.

8. At the same time nationalists look increasingly beyond Africa for support—to India, Egypt and the Arab world; to the USA and the USSR (in varying degrees) and the United Nations. On their side these 'non-colonial' Powers are developing more conscious and positive African policies.

9. Communism is not as yet an effective force within the African national movements, whose leadership is predominantly middle-class, both in social background and outlook. In French West Africa, the French Cameroons and the Sudan, Marxist ideas and Communist groups have some influence, mainly within the trade-union move-

ments—but not elsewhere. There are, however, undoubtedly factors in the African situation which could assist the growth of Communism as an organised force—increasing proletarianisation, land-hunger, economic differentiation among the peasantry, the denial of constitutional channels for nationalist agitation with military and police repression, corruption and inefficiency on the part of the new nationalist governments, the use of African territory and resources to forward the military plans of the Western Powers, etc.

10. The transfer of political power from Europeans to Africans will not, of course, by itself solve any of Africa's basic economic and social problems—nor do serious nationalists believe that it will. Their belief is rather that it is a necessary precondition for the solution of these problems. They are no more prepared than other nationalists in history to accept the conventional colonial argument that economic and social improvement (e.g. increased literacy, a reduction in disease and mortality, advances in agricultural techniques, etc.) must be regarded as a precondition for the transfer of power.

11. The European ascendancy in Africa is not likely to make itself more acceptable to nationalists simply by the device of inventing a new terminology with which to describe itself—*Eurafrique, La Communauté Belgo-Congolaise,* 'Partnership', 'the Multi-racial State', and the like. Nationalists may tend to concentrate too exclusively upon the political problem; but this generally implies an acute awareness of the realities of political power.

12. The weakening, or actual elimination, of the colonial administrative system is liable to produce a situation in which, for a time at any rate, fissiparous tendencies assert themselves, and there is competition for political power between hitherto quiescent groups. These

groups may be organised—as in Ashanti, the three regions of Nigeria, Buganda, or the southern Sudan—around tribal ties and sentiments; and may be led, in name or in fact, by traditional tribal authorities. Loyalties which have their roots in religious sentiments or a rudimentary class consciousness (again the Sudan is an example) may also stimulate opposition to a centralising national government. Yet another disintegrating factor is the arbitrary nature of most colonial frontiers, which may (as in Togoland and the Cameroons) be questioned by revisionist movements, once the withdrawal of the colonial Powers that imposed and maintained them becomes probable. These strains may give rise to demands for looser federal forms of government, or confederations, or eventually to an actual revision of frontiers. There is, however, no ground for supposing that, by prolonging the period of colonial rule, such strains can be mitigated or removed.

13. Recognition that the period of European ascendancy in Africa is drawing to an end, and concentration upon the problem how to ensure that its end does not inflict avoidable suffering, upon Africans, Asians, or Europeans, would seem to be the only rational basis of policy for Britain or any other colonial Power. Such a policy—while it would necessarily imply adaptation on the part of resident non-African minorities to the new situation—need not mean the breaking or weakening of trade or cultural connections between Europe and Africa, or a lessening of African interest in securing the co-operation of European specialists. It might well in fact stimulate this kind of interchange.

# NOTES ON SOURCES

The following notes are as brief as possible. For the most part I have only referred to reasonably accessible literature. Page references are only mentioned where these are likely to be especially useful. Where (as frequently happens) I have referred to the same source more than once in the same chapter, I have used the same number in the text to indicate the later references. Sources on which I have drawn particularly heavily, or which are likely to be of particular interest to the reader, are marked with an asterisk.

## Introductory

1. J. A. HOBSON, *Imperialism.* (1902.)
2. SIR NORMAN ANGELL, *The Great Illusion* (1910), etc.
3. LORD LUGARD, *The Dual Mandate in Tropical Africa.* (1929.)
4. LORD HAILEY, *African Survey.* (1938; revised edition to be published shortly.)
5. See especially MARGERY PERHAM, *Native Administration in Nigeria.* (1937.)
6. For a lucid contemporary restatement of the problem, see PAUL HENRY, *The European Heritage* (in GROVE HAINES, *Africa To-day,* 1955).
7. P. D. BROADBENT, *Sudanese Self-Government.* (International Affairs, XXX, 4, Oct. 1954.) See also SIR HAROLD MACMICHAEL, *The Sudan.* (1954), Part III and Appendix.
8. SYLVIA PANKHURST, *Ethiopia and Eritrea.* (1953.)
9. *Gold Coast (Constitution) Order in Council, 1954.* (See also *Gold Coast: The Government's Proposals for Constitutional Reform, 1953.*)
10. *Nigeria (Constitution) Order in Council, 1954.*
11. United Nations Trusteeship Council. *Visiting Mission's Report on the Trust Territory of Somaliland, 1954.*
12. See for example, *Politique Étrangère, XIX, 4, Oct. 1954.*
13. EDWARD ROUX, *Time Longer Than Rope.* (1948.)

14. Cmd. 9028. Uganda Protectorate: *Withdrawal of Recognition from Kabaka, Mutesa II, of Buganda.* (1953.)

15. Belgian Ministère des Colonies. *La Réorganisation Politique Indigène du Ruanda-Urundi.* (1952.) (See also AUDREY RICHARDS, *Economic Development and Tribal Change,* 1954.)

16. United Nations. *Special Study on Educational Conditions in Non-Self-Governing Territories.* (1954), Ch. 6.

17. For a preliminary study of this topic, see P. GARIGUE, *Changing Political Leadership in West Africa.* (Africa, XXIV, 3, July 1954.)

18. ELSPETH HUXLEY, *White Man's Country.* (1953), I, p. vii.

19. E.g., G. ANTONIUS, *The Arab Awakening* (1938); A. HOURANI, *Syria and the Lebanon* (1946); G. McT. KAHIN, *Nationalism and Revolution in Indonesia* (1952).

20. P. ALDUY, *La Naissance du Nationalisme Outre-Mer* (in Colston Papers, *Principles and Methods of Colonial Administration,* 1950).

21. J. L. and B. HAMMOND, *The Age of the Chartists.* (1930.)

22. Royal Institute of International Affairs. *Nationalism.* (1939.)

23. See *J. S. COLEMAN, *Nationalism in Tropical Africa* (American Political Science Review, XLVIII, 2, June 1954).

24. G. REECE, *The Horn of Africa* (International Affairs, XXX, 4, Oct. 1954).

25. U.N. Trusteeship Council. *Special Report of the First Visiting Mission to Togoland on the Ewe Problem, 1950,* and *Special Report of the U.N. Visiting Mission to Trust Territories in West Africa, 1952, on the Ewe and Togoland Unification Problem.*

26. *G. BALANDIER, *Messianismes et Nationalismes en Afrique Noire.* (Cahiers Internationaux de Sociologie, XIV, 1953.)

27. R. MONTAGNE, *The 'Modern State' in Africa and Asia,* (Cambridge Journal, V, 10, July 1952.)

28. *G. BALANDIER, *Contribution à l'Étude des Nationalismes en Afrique Noire.* (Zaïre, VIII, 4, April 1954.)

29. K. E. ROBINSON, *French Africa and the French Union* (in GROVE HAINES, *Africa To-day,* 1955).

### I. *Policies of the Powers*

1. Comparative studies of colonial policies in Africa can be found in *BUELL, *The Native Problem in Africa* (1928); L. P. MAIR, *Native Policies in Africa* (1936); HAILEY, *African Survey* (1938); and RIIA, *Colonial Administration by European Powers* (1947).

2. LORD HAILEY, *Post-War Changes in Africa*. (Colonial Review, IX, 2, June 1955.) For more detailed information, see UN, *The Enlargement of the Exchange Economy in Tropical Africa* (1954), and RENÉ LAURE, *Le Continent Africain au Milieu du Siècle* (1952).

3. UN, *Summary of Recent Economic Developments in Africa, 1952–3.* (1954.)

4. MARGARET READ, *Education in Africa: Its Pattern and Role in Social Change.* (Colonial Review, IX, 2, June 1955.) See also I. 16.

5. PEP, *Colonial Students in Britain.* (1955.) (See also Présence Africaine, 14, *Les Étudiants Noirs Parlent*, 1954.)

6. Cmd. 9515, *Inter-University Council for Higher Education Overseas, 1946–54.*

7. UN, *Special Study on Social Conditions in Non-Self-Governing Territories.* (1953.)

8. For an official account of Portuguese policy, see MARCELO CAETANO, *Principles and Methods of Portuguese Colonial Administration* (in Colston Papers, cited above).

9. *K. E. ROBINSON, *Political Development in French West Africa* (in CALVIN STILLMAN, *Africa in the Modern World*, 1955) contains the best short account of post-1945 constitutional changes.

10. BUELL, *op. cit.*, I, p. 947.

11. The best-informed discussion in English of French pre-war colonial policy in Africa is DELAVIGNETTE, *Freedom and Authority in French West Africa.* For a useful critical summary of the Brazzaville Decisions, see J. AUBAME, *La Conférence de Brazzaville* (in L'Encyclopédie Coloniale et Maritime, *Afrique Equatoriale Française*, 1950). The best general study of French West

Africa is J. RICHARD-MOLARD, *Afrique Occidentale Française.*

12. C. CORBY, *Une Assemblée Locale dans l'Union Française, le Grand Counseil de l'AOF.* (L'Afrique et L'Asie, 22, 1953.)

13. On FIDES and economic policy in French Africa, see *L'Économie de l'Union Française d'Outre-Mer.* (Recueil Sirey.)

14. P. RIVIERE, *Labour Code for French African Territories.* (International Labour Review, LXVIII, 3, Sept. 1953.)

15. *Journal Officiel,* 19th Nov. 1955 (citing Law of 18th Nov. 1955).

16. G. GAYET, *Évolution Récente des Collèges Electoraux en Afrique Occidentale.* (Académie des Sciences Coloniales, XII, Feb. 1952.)

17. *RENÉ SERVOISE, *Introduction aux Problèmes de la République Française.* (Politique *Étrangère*, XIX, 4, Oct. 1954.)

18. E. W. EVANS, *Principles and Methods of Administration in the British Colonial Empire.* (Colston Papers.)

19. Colonial No. 231, *Report of the[Watson] Commission of Enquiry into Disturbances in the Gold Coast, 1948.*

20. K. E. ROBINSON, *Indirect Rule and Local Government.* (Journal of African Administration, IV, 1, Jan. 1951.)

21. J-L. SIMONET, *L'Évolution Institutionelle dans les Territoires Britanniques de l'Afrique et de l'Ouest.* (Politique Étrangère, XIX, 4, Oct. 1954.)

22. EDMUND BURKE, *Reflections on the French Revolution.*

23. Compare the discussion of this question in J. S. COLEMAN, *Nationalism in Tropical Africa.* (American Political Science Review, XLVIII, 2, June 1954.)

24. For an admirably thorough account of the Native Authority system, see HAILEY, *Native Administration in the British African Territories* (1950).

25. Nuffield Foundation and Colonial Office, *African Education.* (1953.)

26. A useful account of developments in Belgian policy up to 1949 is given in J. J. MAQUET, *Modern Evolution of African Populations in the Belgian Congo.* (Africa, XIX, 4, Oct. 1949.) For the more recent period, see

A. F. G. MARZORATI, *The Belgian Congo* (African Affairs, LIII, 231, April 1954) and G. MALENGREAU, *Recent Developments in Belgian Africa* (in GROVE HAINES, *Africa To-day*).

27. *G. MALENGREAU, *Some Current Problems of Native Policy in the Belgian Congo.* (1954, unpublished.)

28. Congo Belge, Conseil de Gouvernement. *Statistiques.* (1955.)

29. On Belgian educational policy, see J. VANHOVE, *L'Oeuvre d'Éducation au Congo Belge et au Ruanda-Urundi.* (*Encyclopédie du Congo Belge, 1953*.)

30. For an interesting discussion of the problem of political advance, see ANTOINE RUBBENS, *L'Apprentissage de la Démocratie au Congo Belge.* (La Revue Politique, III, 6, Dec. 25th, 1953.)

31. The complicated history of the Sohier Committee and its consequences is explained in G. MALENGREAU, *Chronique de Politique Indigène.* (Zaïre, VI, 9, Nov. 1952.)

32. UN Trusteeship Council, *Visiting Mission's Report on the Trust Territory of Ruanda-Urundi, 1954.*

33. See VERNON MCKAY, *The Impact of the United Nations upon Africa* (in GROVE HAINES, *Africa To-day*).

## II. 1. *The New Towns*

1. See *BOVILL, *Caravans of the Old Sahara* (1933); C. MONTEIL, *Djénné: Une Cité Soudanaise* (1932); and articles by R. MAUNY in the Bulletin de l'IFAN—e.g. on Gao (XIII, 3, July 1951) and Timbuktu (XIV, 3, July 1952).

2. J. RICHARD-MOLARD, *Villes d'Afrique Noire.* (Présence Africaine, No. 15, *Hommage à Jacques Richard-Molard*, 1954.)

3. F. ENGELS, *Condition of the Working-Class in England in 1844.*

4. J. LOMBARD, *Cotonou, Ville Africaine.* (Bulletin de l'IFAN, XVI, 3–4, July/October 1954.)

5. *G. BALANDIER, *Approche Sociologique des 'Brazzavilles Noires'.* (Africa, XXII, 1, Jan. 1952.)

6. PAUL HENRY, *The European Heritage* (in GROVE HAINES, *Africa To-day*).

7. I. A. HASSOUN, *'Western' Migration and Settlement in

the Gezira. (Sudan Notes and Records, XXXIII, 1, June 1952.)

8.  J. GUILBOT, Petite Étude sur la Main-d'œuvre à Douala. (Centre IFAN, Cameroun, Memo. 1, 1948.)

9.  J.-P. LEBEUF, Bangui, Oubangui-Chari. (Editions de l'Union Français, 1953.)

10. G. BALANDIER, Travail Non-Salarié dans les Brazzavilles Noires. (Zaïre, VI, 7, July 1952.)

11. *G. BALANDIER, Sociologie des Brazzavilles Noires. (1955.)

12. G. SAUTTER, L'Exode vers les Grands Centres en AEF (unpublished paper). See also his article, Aperçu sur les Villes 'Africaines' du Moyen-Congo, in L'Afrique et l'Asie, 14, 1951. I am indebted to M. Sautter for the quotations in the following paragraph, and for much valuable material that I have made use of elsewhere in this chapter.

13. M. GOSSELIN, Bamako, Ville Soudanaise. (L'Afrique et l'Asie, 21, 1953.)

14. J. DRESCH, Villes d'Afrique Occidentale. (Cahiers d'Outre-Mer, III, 11, July/Oct. 1950.) A useful short comparative study of the physical and social characteristics of a number of West African towns.

15. J. DRESCH, Villes Congolaises. (Revue de Géographie Humaine et d'Ethnologie, I, 3, July/Sept. 1948.)

16. P. MERCIER, Aspects de la Société Africaine dans l'Agglomération Dakaroise. (IFAN, Études Sénéga-laises, No. 5, 1954.)

17. BOVILL, op. cit., p. 57.

18. DAVID DIOP, quoted from L. S. SENGHOR's anthology, La Nouvelle Poésie Nègre et Malgache. (1948.)

19. E. S. MUNGER, Geography of Sub-Saharan Race Relations (in GROVE HAINES, Africa To-day).

20. *K. A. BUSIA, Social Survey of Sekondi-Takoradi. (1950.)

21. B. B. BADIE, Le Sort du Travailleur Noir de Côte d'Ivoire. (In Présence Africaine, No. 13, Le Travail en Afrique Noire, 1952.)

22. G. BALANDIER, Le Travailleur Africain dans les 'Brazza-ville Noires'. (In Le Travail en Afrique Noire.)

23. For an interesting description of this aspect of town life,

see CYPRIAN EKWENSI'S novel, *People of the City* (set in Lagos).

24. J. L. and B. HAMMOND, *The Age of the Chartists*, p. 16.

25. P. MERCIER, *L'Affaiblissement des Processus d' Intégration dans les Sociétés en Changement.* (Bulletin de l'IFAN, XVI, 1–2, Jan./April 1954.)

26. J. D. RHEINALLT JONES, *Effects of Urbanization in South and Central Africa.* (African Affairs, LII, 206, Jan. 1953.)

27. See below, ch. III. 6.

28. P. E. H. HAIR, *An Industrial and Urban Community in East Nigeria [Enugu], 1914–53.* (WAISER Conference Proceedings, Sociology Section, Ibadan, 1953.)

29. BONIFACE MWÉPU, *La Vie des Femmes Legères, dites 'Libres', au C. E. C. d'Elisabethville.* (CEPSI, No. 17, 1953.)

## II. 2. *The New Associations*

1. On modern associations in general, see *KENNETH LITTLE, *The Study of 'Social Change' in British West Africa* (Africa, XXIII, 4, Oct. 1953), and *Structural Change in the Sierra Leone Protectorate* (Africa, XXV, 3, July 1955); also DARYLL FORDE, *The Conditions of Social Development in West Africa* (Civilisations, III, 4, 1953, p. 581).

2. On the importance of Burial Clubs, see K. A. BUSIA, *Social Survey of Sekondi-Takoradi*, pp. 77–83 and 111–12.

3. LORD HAILEY, *Native Administration in the British African Territories*, III, p. 19.

4. S. OTTENBERG, *Improvement Associations among the Afikpo Ibo.* (Africa, XXV, 1, Jan. 1955.) This article contains a useful bibliography on tribal or 'improvement' associations.

5. J.-P. LEBEUF, *Bangui, Oubangui-Chari.*

6. G. BALANDIER, *Approche Sociologique des 'Brazzavilles Noires'* III. 15. See also III. 1. 11.

7. J. S. COLEMAN, *The Role of Tribal Associations in Nigeria.* (WAISER Conference Proceedings, Ibadan, 1952.)

8. An excellent account of the activities of the *Cercles Culturels* of French Equatorial Africa is to be found in their monthly journal, *Liaison*, published in Brazzaville.

9. *SA'AD-ED-DIN FAWZI, *The Origins and Development of the Labour Movement in the Sudan*. (Unpublished thesis.)

10. U.N. Trusteeship Council, *Visiting Mission's Report on the Trust Territory of Togoland, under French Administration, 1953.*

11. *B. HOLAS, *La Goumbé*. (Kongo-Overzee. XIX, 2–3, 1953.)

12. MARGERY PERHAM, *Native Administration in Nigeria.*

13. R. K. GARDINER and H. O. JUDD, *The Development of Social Administration.* (1954.)

14. Egba Women's Union, *The Fall of a Ruler, or the Freedom of Egbaland.* (n.d.)

15. J. L. and B. HAMMOND, *The Age of the Chartists.*

## II. 3. *Prophets and Priests*

1. Two articles by F. A. MUSGROVE, *Uganda Secondary School as a field of Cultural Change* and *Education and the Culture Concept* (Africa, XXII, 3, July 1952, and XXIII, 2, April 1953), throw some light on the second question. A. T. PORTER, *Religious Affiliation in Freetown, Sierra Leone* (Africa, XXIII, 1, Jan. 1953), discusses the question of the social influence of the Mission Churches.

2. For the opposition to traditionalism in Islam, see *A. LE GRIP, *Aspects Actuels de l'Islam en AOF* (L'Afrique et L'Asie, 24, 1953, and 25, 1954). On Mahdism, see M. LE GRIP'S article in the same journal (18, 1952), *Le Mahdisme en Afrique Noire*. A. GOUILLY, *L'Islam en AOF* (1952), and J. SPENCER TRIMINGHAM, *Islam in the Sudan* (1949), are also relevant.

3. See K. A. BUSIA, *Social Survey of Sekondi-Takoradi*; B. HOLAS, *Bref Aperçu sur les Principaux Cultes Syncrétiques de la Basse Côte d'Ivoire* (Africa, XXIV, 1, Jan. 1954); L. S. B. Leakey, *Defeating Mau-Mau* (1954), chs. 4 and 5; and, for an earlier period, E. DE JONGHE, *Formations Récentes de Sociétés Sécrétes au Congo*

*Belge* (Africa, IX, 1, Jan. 1936). A useful introduction
to the whole subject is HUBERT DESCHAMPS, *Les Reli-
gions de l'Afrique Noire (Que Sais-je?* No. 632, 1954).

4. For the Donatists, and successor sects, see MGR. RONALD
KNOX, *Enthusiasm.* (1951.)

5. *DARYLL FORDE (ed.), *African Worlds.* (1954.)

6. *G. BALANDIER, *Messianismes et Nationalismes en
Afrique Noire.* (I. 27 above.)

7. ROLAND OLIVER, *The Missionary Factor in East Africa*
(1952), p. 185.

8. *B. G. M. SUNDKLER, *Bantu Prophets in South Africa.*
(1948.) As will be evident, I have drawn heavily on Dr.
Sundkler's classic study throughout this chapter.

9. *R. L. BUELL, *The Native Problem in Africa,* II, ch. 94.

10. W. BASCOM, *African Culture and the Missionary.* (Civilisations, III, 4, 1953.) The quotation is from an Angola
journal.

11. G. PARRINDER, *Religion in an African City* (1953), ch. 6.

12. *G. SHEPPERSON, *The Politics of African Church
Separatist Movements in British Central Africa.*
(Africa, XXIV, 3, July 1954.)

13. G. SHEPPERSON, *Ethiopianism and African Nationalism.*
(Phylon, XIV, 1, 1953.) This article gives a useful list
of sources for 'Ethiopianism' and the influence of
American Negro Churches on African separatist movements.

14. See references to the Garvey movement in BUELL, *op. cit.*
E. D. CRONON's *Black Moses* (University of Wisconsin
Press, 1955) is the first full-length biography of Marcus
Garvey.

15. I owe this point, and other helpful suggestions regarding
this chapter, to Mr. George Shepperson.

16. A. OLONIO, *Church Marriages in Nigeria.* (n.d.)

17. L. MQOTSI and N. MKELE, *A Separatist Church: Ibandla
lika-Kristu.* (African Studies, V, 2, June 1946.)

18. In the remainder of this chapter the main sources for the
various prophet movements referred to are as follows:

(*a*) For Shembe and the Nazarites—B. G. M. SUNDKLER,
*op. cit.*

(*b*) For Harris and Harrism—R. L. BUELL, *op. cit.,* for the earlier period, and B. HOLAS, *op. cit.*, for recent developments.

(c) For Kimbanguism, Kakism and Matswanism—G. BALANDIER, *op. cit.*, and *Sociologie Actualle de l'Afrique Noire* (1955).

(d) For the Watchtower Movement and *Kitawala*—I. CUNNISON, *The Watchtower Assembly in Central Africa* (International Review of Missions, XL, 160, Oct. 1951); J. L. COMHAIRE, *Sociétés Sécrètes et Mouvements Prophétiques au Congo Belge* (Africa, XXV, 1, Jan. 1955).

(e) For Masinde and *Dina Ya Misambwa*—L. C. USHERWILSON, *Dina Ya Misambwa* (Uganda Journal, XVI, 2, Sept. 1952).

(f) For *Watu Wa Mngu*—J. KENYATTA, *Facing Mount Kenya* (1953), ch. 11.

(On all these see also the summary in H. DÉSCHAMPS, *op. cit.*)

19. WILLIAM PRYNNE, *Anti-Arminianism.* (1630.) (Quoted in A. S. P. WOODHOUSE, *Puritanism and Liberty*, 1938.)

20. J. S. TRIMINGHAM, *Islam in the Sudan*, p. 148.

21. A. LE GRIP, *Le Mahdisme en Afrique Noire.* See also KATESA SCHLOSSER, *Propheten in Afrika.* (1949.)

## II. 4. *Workers and Peasants*

1. For the rise of an African middle class, see ASSANÉ SECK, *Le Formation d'une Classe Moyenne en AOF*, and C. C. WRIGLEY, *The Development of a Middle Class in British East Africa* (working papers for the 29th Study Session of INCIDI, London, Sept. 1955); also P. C. LLOYD, *New Economic Classes in Western Nigeria* (African Affairs, LII, 209, Oct. 1953); and articles by KENNETH LITTLE referred to under III, 2 (1).

2. F. J. AMON D'ABY, *La Côte d'Ivoire dans la Cité Africaine* (1951), pp. 110–14.

3. Union of Democratic Control, *African Conference Report, October 1950* (duplicated).

4. The table in the text has been conflated mainly from the following sources: *Bulletin of the Inter-African Labour Institute, Oct. 31st, 1953; U.N. Enlargement of the Ex-*

*change Economy in Tropical Africa* (1954); *Note sur le Syndicalisme en Afrique Noire* in *Le Travail en Afrique Noire* (Présence Africaine 1952); WALTER BOWN, *Colonial Trade Unions* (Fabian Colonial Bureau, 1954); and territorial annual reports.

5. G. BALANDIER, *Le Developpement Industriel et le Proletarianisation en Afrique Noire.* (L'Afrique et l'Asie, 20, 1952.)

6. International Labour Office Report V (1), *Migrant Workers (Undeveloped Countries).* (1953.)

7. C. H. NORTHCOTT, *African Labour Efficiency Survey.* (Colonial Research Publications, No. 31, 1949.)

8. SA'AD-ED-DIN FAWZI, *The Origins and Development of the Labour Movement in the Sudan.* (Most of the material on the Sudan in this chapter is derived from Sa'ad-ed-din Fawzi's excellent unpublished study.)

9. B. GUSSMAN, *Industrial Efficiency and the Urban African.* (Africa, XXIII, 2, April 1953.)

10. Government of Northern Rhodesia, *Report of Board of Inquiry on the Advancement of Africans in the Copper Mining Industry in Northern Rhodesia.* (1954.)

11. G. BALANDIER, *Le Travailleur Africain dans les 'Brazzavilles Noires'* (in *Le Travail en Afrique Noire*).

12. J. L. and B. HAMMOND, *The Age of the Chartists*, p. 27. On the contrast between the old rhythm and the new discipline, see A. S. TIDJANI, *L'Africain Face au Problème du Travail* (in *Le Travail en Afrique Noire*).

13. *A. HAUSER, *Quelques Relations des Travailleurs de l'Industrie à leur Travail en AOF.* (Bulletin de l'IFAN, XVII, 1–2, Jan./April 1955.)

14. R. E. LUYT, *Trade Unionism in African Colonies.* (South African Institute of Race Relations, 1949.)

15. See BASIL DAVIDSON, *African Awakening* (1955).

16. R. A. BRADY, *Business as a System of Power* (1943), ch. 8.

17. M. G. H. CONNILLIERE, *Training of Workers in French Equatorial Africa.* (Translated in the Inter-African Labour Institute Bulletin, IX, Sept. 1954.)

18. Union Minière du Haut-Katanga, *Exercice 1952: Statistiques et Commentaires.* (1953.)

19. R. L. BUELL, *The Native Problem in Africa*, I, pp. 887–90.

20. EDWARD ROUX, *Time Longer Than Rope*. (1948.)

21. See BUELL, *op. cit.*, for information regarding these early strikes, and Cmd. 5009, *Report of the Commission appointed to enquire into the Disturbances in the Copperbelt, Northern Rhodesia*. (1935.)

22. GUY MALENGREAU, *Recent Developments in Belgian Africa* (in GROVE HAINES, *Africa To-day*, p. 351).

23. J. I. ROPER and R. B. DAVIDSON, *The Labour and Trade Union Ordinances of the Gold Coast*. (West African Affairs, No. 15.)

24. P. HUGUET, *Code du Travail d'Outre-Mer*. (1953.)

25. G. ST. J. ORDE BROWNE, *Labour Conditions in West Africa*. (Cmd. 6277, 1941.)

26. *P. C. LLOYD, *Craft Organisation in Yoruba Towns*. (Africa, XXIII, 1, Jan. 1953.)

27. *Labour Administration in the Colonial Territories, 1944-50*. (Colonial No. 275, 1951.)

28. For French African Trade Unionism, see *Note sur le Syndicalisme en Afrique Noire* (4 above), and J. LECAILLON, *Les Incidences Economiques et Financières du Code du Travail* (*Institut des Hautes Études, Dakar, 1954*); also A. HAUSER, *op. cit.*, and references in *Marchés Coloniaux* and *Afrique-Informations*.

29. W. TUDOR DAVIES, *Enquiry into the Cost of Living in Nigeria*. (Colonial No. 204, 1946, pp. 2-3.)

30. WALTER BOWN, *op. cit.*

31. J. LECAILLON, *op. cit.*

32. J. L. COMHAIRE, *Sociétés Sécrètes et Mouvements Prophétiques au Congo Belge*. (Cited in III. 3, 18 above.)

33. Afrique-Informations (1954), Nos. 17-18, *Les Grèves en AOF*.

34. Gouvernement-General de l'AOF, Territoire du Soudan Français: *Conventions Collectives, Chauffeurs Africains*. (1952.)

35. B. G. PONOUKOUN, *La Vie d'un Militant Syndicaliste* (in *Le Travail en Afrique Noire*).

36. Colonial No. 256, *Report of the Commission of Enquiry into the Disorders in the Eastern Provinces of Nigeria, Nov. 1949*. (1950.)

## II. 5. *Parties and Congresses*

1. *M. DUVERGER, *Political Parties* (1954). An admirable study, of which I have made frequent use in this chapter.

2. M. WIGHT, *The Gold Coast Legislative Council* (1947), pp. 74–75 and 184.

3. G. PADMORE, *The Gold Coast Revolution.* (1953), pp. 36–47.

4. R. BUELL, *The Native Problem in Africa*, I, ch. 45.

5. There is unfortunately no published account of the pre-war development of the SFIO in Senegal. I have depended mainly upon oral tradition and references in the post-war SFIO's monthly *Bulletin Intérieur*.

6. MEKKI ABBAS, *The Sudan Question.* (1952.)

7. F. M. BOURRET, *The Gold Coast.* (1949), pp. 43–4. See also (2) and (3).

8. OKOI ARIKPO, *The Protest Movement in West Africa.* (London School of Economics Seminar Paper: duplicated.)

9. JOAN WHEARE, *The Nigerian Legislative Council.* (1950), ch. 3.

10. Cmd. 5845, *Report on the Marketing of West African Cocoa.* (1938.) See also (7).

11. See particularly Colonial No. 231, *Report of the [Watson] Commission of Enquiry into Disturbances in the Gold Coast, 1948.*

12. ASA BRIGGS, *People and Constitution in the Gold Coast: 4, The Role of Political Parties.* (West Africa, March 29th, 1952.)

13. *The Constitution of the National Council of Nigeria and the Cameroons* (1945). See also HAILEY, *Native Administrations in the British African Territories*, Part III, pp. 21–2.

14. *Le Rassemblement Démocratique Africain dans la Lutte Anti-imperialiste.* (1948.)

15. G. D'ARBOUSSIER, *La Situation Actuelle du RDA* (1948) in *Le RDA dans la Lutte Anti-imperialiste.*

16. See particularly Sir Hugh Clifford, quoted in WHEARE, *op. cit.*, pp. 31–2.

17. D. COLE, *How Strong is the African National Congress?* (New Commonwealth, XXVII, 1, Jan. 4th, 1954.)

18. L. S. B. LEAKEY, *Mau-Mau and the Kikuyu* (1952), ch. 10. See also MONTAGUE SLATER, *The Trial of Jomo Kenyatta* (1955).

19. *J. S. COLEMAN, *The Emergence of African Political Parties* (in GROVE HAINES, *Africa To-day*).

20. G. GAYET, *Évolution Récente des Collèges Électoraux en Afrique Occidentale.* (1952. (II. 16. above.)

21. G. D'ARBOUSSIER, *Lettre Ouverte* and *Deuxième Lettre Ouverte à Félix Houphouet-Boigny*; and F. HOUPHOUET-BOIGNY, *Réponse à D'Arboussier* (in the journal, *Afrique Noire*, 24th July 1952).

22. F. F. AMON D'ABY, *La Côte d'Ivoire dans la Cité Africaine.*

23. For an interesting statement of Mr. Awolowo's political philosophy, see his book, *Path to Nigerian Freedom*, (1947.)

24. See especially FILY DABO SISSOKO, *Le Socialisme et L'Afrique* (Bulletin Intévieur du Parti Socialiste SFIO, 56, June 1951).

25. On 'partis de l'Administration' in French Togoland, see Afrique-Informations, No. 35–6, April/May 1955, *Le Problème Politique du Togo.*

26. J. DELVAL, *Le RDA au Soudan Français.* (L'Afrique et l'Asie, 16, 1951.)

27. *Statuts de BDS.* See also L. S. SENGHOR, *La Méthode et la Doctrine du Bloc Démocratique Sénégalais.* (Marchés Coloniaux, March 27th, 1954.)

28. For an example of such a 'linked' organisation see B. HOLAS, *La Goumbé* (III. 2. 11. above).

29. Afrique-Informations, 34, March/April 1955: *Incidents en Guinée Française, 1954–1955.*

30. On French West African party alignments, see K. E. ROBINSON, *Political Development in French West Africa* (in CALVIN STILLMAN, *Africa in the Modern World*, 1955).

(In addition to the sources listed here the weekly journal *West Africa* has published a large number of articles over the past few years, dealing with party organisation and party relationships, mainly in the British West African territories.)

## II. 6. *Theories and Myths*

1. Quoted in L. S. B. LEAKEY, *Defeating Mau-Mau.*
2. Dr. Richard Price's Old Jewry sermon (1789), quoted in H. N. BRAILSFORD, *Shelley, Godwin and their Circle.* (1936.)
3. MARGARET READ, *Cultural Contacts in Education.* (Paper read to the British Association, Education Section, Edinburgh, 1951.)
4. H. MARTIN, *Pays Bamum et Sultan Njoya.* (IFAN, Études Camerounaises, 4, 33–4, Sept./Dec. 1951.) See also M. LITTLEWOOD, *Peoples of the Central Cameroons* (International African Institute, Ethnographic Survey of Africa, 1954), pp. 56–7.
5. CASELY HAYFORD, *Gold Coast Native Institutions.* (1903.)
6. M. WIGHT, *The Gold Coast Legislative Council.*
7. E.g., SIR PHILIP MITCHELL, *Africa and the West in Historical Perspective* (in GROVE HAINES, *Africa Today*).
8. CHEIKH ANTA DIOP, *Nations Nègres et Cultures.* (1954.)
9. For sources, see DIEDRICH WESTERMANN , *Geschichte Afrikas* (1952), and SOAS, *History and Archaeology in Africa* (1955).
10. E. W. BOVILL, *Caravans of the Old Sahara*, ch. 7.
11. FELIX DUBOIS, *Timbuctoo the Mysterious.* (1897), ch. 13.
12. FILY-DABO SISSOKO, *Les Noirs et la Culture.* (1950.)
13. See, for example, the publications of Présence Africaine, particularly *Le Monde Noir* and *L'Art Nègre.*
14. THOMAS HOBBES, *Leviathan*, Part I, ch. 13.
15. SIR APOLO KAGWA, *Ekitabo Kya Basekabaka.*
16. S. JOHNSON, *History of the Yorubas.* (1921.)
17. J. M. SARBAH, *Fanti Customary Laws* (1897), and *The Fanti National Constitution* (1906).
18. J. B. DANQUAH, *The Akan Doctrine of God.* (1944.)
19. A. KAGAMÉ, *Bref Aperçu sur la Poésie Dynastique du Rwanda.* (Zaïre, IV, 3, March 1950.)
20. For a summary of existing knowledge about the kingdom of Ghana, see R. A. MAUNY, *The Question of Ghana* (Africa, XXIV, 3, July 1954)

21. E. E. Asamoa, *The Problem of Language in Education in the Gold Coast*. (Africa, XXV, 1, Jan. 1955.)

22. J-P. Sartre, *Orphée Noir* (*Preface to* L-S. Senghor, *La Nouvelle Poésie Nègre et Malgache*).

23. G. McT. Kahin, *Nationalism and Revolution in Indonesia*, p. 49.

24. G. Shepperson, *Ethiopianism and African Nationalism* (and suggestions made in correspondence).

25. An interesting first-hand account of the various Pan-African Congresses held from 1919 on is to be found in W. E. B. Du Bois, *The World and Africa* (1947), pp. 7–12 and 235–45.

26. Maghemout Diop, *L'Unique Issue: L'Indépendance Totale* (in *Les Étudiants Noirs Parlent*). (II. 5, above.)

27. L.-S. Senghor, *Ce que l'Afrique Attend de l'Europe*. (Marchés Coloniaux, May 14th, 1955.)

28. E.g. Albert Franklin, *Négritude—Réalité ou Mystification?* (in *Les Étudiants Noirs Parlent*).

# INDEX